THE CARS AND THE FACTORY

Titles in the Crowood AutoClassics Series

THE CARS AND THE FACTORY

JOHN TIPLER

First published in 1993 by
The Crowood Press Ltd
Ramsbury, Marlborough
Wiltshire SN8 2HR

British Library Cataloguing-in-Publication Data

A catalogue record for this book is available from the British
Library.

ISBN   1 85223 750 3

Picture Credits

Line-drawings on pages 13, 26 and 45 by Bob Constant; other
artwork supplied by Morgan Motor Company.

Typeset by Chippendale Type Ltd, Otley, West Yorkshire.
Printed and bound in Great Britain by BPCC Hazells Ltd.
Member of BPCC Ltd.

Contents

Acknowledgements

When I set out to write this book, I was apprehensive that I would be greeted with a big yawn at Malvern. 'Oh no, not another book about Morgan!' I thought they would say. But not a bit of it. When I explained that what Crowood Press wanted was a comprehensive job on the build process, I was welcomed heartily. So I am extremely grateful to everyone who provided me with information at the factory, starting with Charles Morgan and his father Peter; who better to write the Foreword than the Production Manager? They lent me a development Plus 4 and the Chairman's own Plus 8 for evaluation while I did much of my research.

I want to credit the foremen of all the different departments, starting with David Day of chassis assembly, Geoff Brewer in sheet metal, Graham Hall in wood and coachbuilding, Derek Gardner in the paint shop, Tony Newman in the machine shop, Charlie Styles on trimming, Don Passey in final assembly, chief tester Tony Monk, development engineer Bill Beck, toolmaker and CAD man Dave Goodwin; and Mark Baldwin in the repair shop.

Many thanks also to Derek Day, Sales Director and Mark Read, Assistant Sales Manager; Buying Director Roger Talbot, Works Manager and Assistant Managing Director Mark Aston; Geoff Margetts, Company Secretary, and Parts Manager Paul Trussler. As 130 people work at Morgan, I could go on a lot longer.

Simon Clay from the National Motor Museum took masses of photographs, patiently hacking through my photo list; racers Bill Wykeham, John McDonald, Rob Wells, Chris Alford, Charles Morgan and rallyist Jane Bourne provided competition pictures. Other photographs came from Neil Miller, a professional photographer from Arizona who took pictures of his own car as it progressed through the factory; Chris Rowe of the Morgan Sports Car Club; Chris Harvey; the Morgan Model Company; and Ken Hill. My old friend Laurie Caddell of CW Editorial came up with some excellent colour transparencies, as did Charles Morgan. Archive pics were provided by the National Motor Museum and the Morgan Motor Company Ltd. Thanks also to *Motor*, *Motor Sport* and *Road and Track* magazines for the road tests. And I want to mention Norfolk cabinet-maker Steve Wiles who gave me some of the background on ash and its uses.

I should like to dedicate the book to Alvary, who I hope will one day be a Plus 4 man!

Foreword

I welcome John Tipler's faithful record of how a Morgan sports car is built, which adds to the growing library of Morgan books. It is illustrated with the photographs of Simon Clay, photographer of the National Motor Museum at Beaulieu. The book is the culmination of months of John's hard work and careful observation at the factory in Malvern. I am very pleased that after all the research his respect for the cars and the people who build them has grown. It is obviously crucial to the company's future that we maintain our standards of craftsmanship and can demonstrate these skills to our customers. I hope that this book shares with a wider audience the methods of coachbuilding quality sports cars.

John's book also demonstrates that in spite of our dedication to traditional skills and standards of quality, there are improvements that are being made to our processes and to the specifications of the cars themselves. If they had been available at the time, the great coachbuilders of the 1920s would undoubtedly have used wood preservatives to make their cars last even longer. Henry Royce would have used a computer box to control the fuel economy and performance of the engine of the Silver Ghost if electronic engine management systems had been invented in 1906. It *is* therefore possible to improve on past standards and our policy is to make changes continually where we can demonstrate that this is genuinely beneficial.

At the same time we are looking to increase our production levels to give more people the opportunity of becoming Morgan owners. This will be a gradual process as the training to become a craftsman in many of the departments of the Morgan factory takes as long as six years. But with demand for the cars showing no signs of slackening, and with our waiting lists growing worldwide, we have to achieve significant production increases and we have shown over the last few years that this is possible.

Whatever we change on the cars or our production processes we will always keep one commitment firmly at the top of the list. That is to make sure that Morgans are a thrill to drive. From the first three-wheeler designed by H. F. S. Morgan in 1909 to the Morgan Plus 8 which celebrates its 25th anniversary in 1993, Morgans have been about enjoying yourself at the wheel of a car. We hope that for many years to come their distinctive shape will brighten up roads around the world and that their drivers will agree with Roger Chapman, the executive director of the Parliamentary Advisory Council for Road Safety, who said, 'Morgans put the motoring back into driving.'

I am sure you will enjoy this book and I would like to thank all of those who contributed to it. All of us at Morgans would also like to thank Morgan owners and enthusiasts for putting so much back into the enjoyment of the marque.

Charles Morgan

Charles Morgan

Family Tree

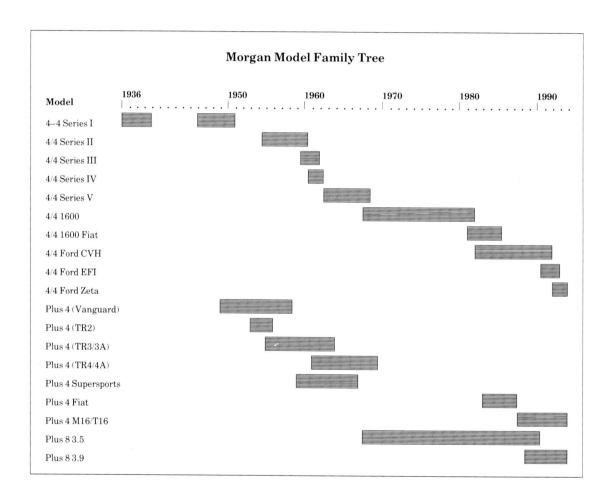

Introduction

Looking back over my years of car owner-ship, hot saloons predominate, from my first motor, a Ford Anglia with a 1,340cc Classic engine, to an Alfa Romeo Giulia 1300 TI whose performance was enlivened with a 2.0-litre motor; sports cars in my life were of the Lotus Elan and MGB/C variety, owned when such models were in current produc-tion. Later on I tried a spot of club racing with a 2.5-litre Alfa GTV6. This is by way of admitting that for me, Morgans were a bit too retro in aspect. An acquaintance in the late 1960s had a Plus 8, and I admired the noise and bravado rather than the lines. When working on the magazine *Restoring Classic Cars* in the late 1980s, I did a feature on off-the-shelf classics, and we were lent a Plus 8 by the factory to trundle round Donington. I was impressed by the power but less enamoured of the handling and the ergonomics.

Then in the early 1990s I had a couple of monthly columns in *Performance Car* maga-zine. One was called 'Driving Month', in which people on the periphery of the motor industry or with a specialist interest in cars talked about topical issues. Charles Morgan was one person on my hit-list, and after we had recorded an interview, he showed me around the factory.

My conception of Morgans changed, and long-held prejudices vanished, because here was a car which was almost bespoke, care-fully coachbuilt on an ash frame by diligent craftsmen in a way I could relate to, using traditional techniques, rather than run off by the thousand by robots. It was a revela-tion. My other column in *Performance Car* was called 'Second Chances', all about

Charles Morgan, Production Manager, joined the family firm in 1983.

buying the car you always promised yourself second-hand. When it came to doing the Morgan, I learned a great deal from John Worrall, proprietor of Heart of England Morgans. He talked me round the cars' shortcomings and showed me where they deteriorate and how to restore the bits that go wrong.

Clearly I had been missing something, for despite the post-war stylistic evolution of sports cars from, let's say, TR2 through E-type to the last Lotus Elan (r.i.p.), and the technical evolution from Lotus 7 through

To dismiss the Morgan shape as retrospective is to overlook the sensuous curves of what is altogether a romantic motor car.

Lotus Elan to BMW Z1, a steady trickle of sporting enthusiasts wanted their cars to be hand-built in this time-honoured fashion. The following chapters will show why they were so astute. Not in the sense of financial speculation, although few cars hold their values so well, but because the Morgan is today a very special car; they don't build 'em like that any more. The Morgan Motor Company is the last of the coachbuilders in the tradition of Thrupp and Maberley, Park Ward and Mulliner, Gurney Nutting or Van den Plas, Hooper or James Young. It is a rather simpler car than the saloons, limousines or sports tourers these firms specialized in, but no less hand crafted. But although it is built in the traditional way, the Morgan frame should not be seen as comparable to something like an MG TC, as the quality of materials and manufacture is many times better; the MG's metal rusted and the wood was not strong enough.

DEMAND

Because it is a slow process, with just ten cars a week being finished, assuming no delays on component supply, there has always been a waiting list. For more than twenty-five years, demand for Morgans has outstripped supply. In the early 1970s, a customer might have expected a three-year wait for his car, but such was the boom in the mid-1970s that it rose to six years. And in 1980 a wait of ten years was talked about. Production rose by one unit to ten cars a week to go a little way towards reducing the backlog of orders, although nowadays an eight-year hiatus is considered normal. Many people saw the *Troubleshooter* series on television in which Sir John Harvey-Jones was asked to comment on how the backlog might be reduced. As I discuss elsewhere, his solutions were not suitable, and Peter and Charles Morgan decided they were better off to maintain the status quo.

As a result of the demand for new cars,

Despite stylistic progression, a steady trickle of fans wanted their cars coachbuilt in the traditional way; there is a timeless quality about the cars, and an outside observer would be hard pressed to date Chris Alford's 4/4 racing exploits to 1975.

some are ordered with a view to being re-sold at a premium on delivery. The profit-takers and investors of the late 1980s classic car boom were deliberately discouraged by the company, who quite correctly saw the basis of their business amongst the middle-class enthusiast, and maintained the prices of its models accordingly. Morgans, after all, are all about an exhilarating driving experi-ence, a far cry from the sordid wrangling of the brokers in the City. Many will argue that the Morgan is an anachronism, with only its engines keeping pace with modern motoring. Morgan may be alive and kicking now, but its image recaptures an epoch when road behaviour was many times better than it is today, when roads were half as crowded, and perhaps there is a secret yearning amongst Morgan owners to be seen as decent chaps harking back to those days. Misty-eyed nostalgia? Perhaps. Others see it as a living classic, parked up alongside the MGB-RV8, Alfa Romeo Spider, Caterham Seven, TVR S3, Porsche 911 if you like, as well as such survivors as the Autokraft AC Cobra, Marcos, Bristol, Jensen and Evante, which are produced in even smaller volumes.

But the point is, does a car necessarily have to change its shape? When Morgan went streamlined with the Plus Four Plus, fans shied away. Motor industry practice has always been to change model styling as regularly as possible. This was a trend insti-gated by the grandfather of styling, Harley Earl, in the mid-1920s to attract new buyers, and brought to a fine art by the Japanese in recent years, who reckon to facelift every two years and go for a comple-tely new shape every four. This has also brought in retro-styling, exemplified by the Panther Kalista, a pastiche which failed because it was not built properly, and certainly not along Morgan principles; a Turkish outfit has come up with a fibreglass replica of a Morgan which will not fool anyone; and there's the Miata MX5, a 1960s Elan lookalike to all intents and purposes. Are these cars amusing, bogus design, or do they simply recognize that it is impossible to improve on a tried and tested formula for the sports car format? Presumably they could not copy the Morgan because it is still in production. And what's more, under that traditional skin, it's continuously evolving.

1 History of Morgan

You come upon the Morgan factory almost by accident. The long, low single-storey red-brick Victorian workshops nestle amongst a post-war housing estate of semi-detached and council houses beside Pickersleigh Road. Malvern Link, a 'suburb' of Malvern, lies on the lower slopes of the majestic Malvern Hills which provide such a splendid backdrop. Poplar trees indicate the factory's border with a neighbouring playing field. Everything about the factory is understated, even down to the visitors' car park at the bottom of the gently sloping site, a small area for perhaps a dozen or so cars. In the yard, men in overalls quite casually push rolling chassis around. There are normally six or seven half-completed cars outside, under wraps if it is raining.

The impression is of a low-key operation. A couple of chassis sit on the ground outside the machine shop, together with half a dozen axles. Round the corner is the wood shed, where planks and blocks of ash sit piled high, curing and waiting for selection for their part in the build process. But what is this? A pair of church pews! Clearly freshly made, the pale ash lacking the patina of use. Can this be the seating for a secret Morgan charabanc, I wonder. Beside them I recognize half a dozen newly-treated Morgan frames, and the air is heavy with the slightly nauseating aroma of Cuprisol. The reason soon becomes clear; behind the wood shed is the dipping tank, where the frames are dunked.

This is something relatively new in Morgan manufacture, for the frame, always vulnerable to wet and dry rot, now has a fighting chance of surviving to a decent old age instead of just a few years if neglected. But when the founder, H. F. S. Morgan, began making his own cars in 1909, coachbuilt wooden vehicles were the order of the day, and carried on being so, especially for

Entrance to the reception area of Morgan's Pickersleigh Road factory.

12

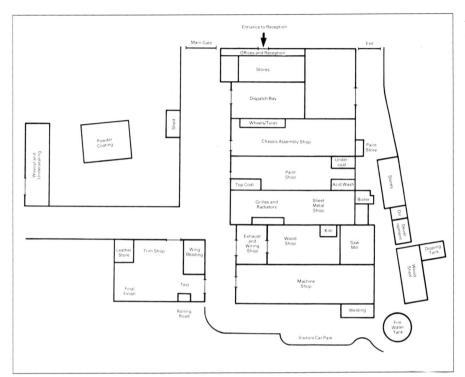

Factory plan, 1993.

bespoke limousines, pretty much until unit-construction in steel became commonplace in the 1960s.

H. F. S. MORGAN

Harry 'HFS' Morgan was born in Hereford-shire on the other side of the Malvern Hills at Stoke Lacey in 1881, where his father George was later the vicar, as had his grand-father been before that. After leaving Marl-borough school, Morgan took a technical rather than an artistic path, and studied at Crystal Palace Engineering College, and armed with a grounding in technical draw-ing, he became an apprentice to the Chief Engineer on the Great Western Railway at Swindon. By coincidence, W.O. Bentley was likewise a railway apprentice, although the two men's products were virtually at oppo-site ends of the vehicular spectrum.

Railways held no thrall, so Morgan opened a garage on Worcester Road, Malvern Link in 1906, selling Darracq and Wolseley cars and operating a regular bus service between Malvern and Worcester, some eight miles away. When this proved unfeasible due to public apathy, he turned to car hire, and between times, built a motorcycle powered by an air-cooled 7hp V-twin Peugeot engine. The next step, in 1909, was to build a three-wheeler, using the same engine mounted out in front of a lightweight tubular frame chas-sis. HFS was given the use of an engineering workshop at Malvern College, and was assisted in his endeavours by the engineer-ing master Mr Stephenson-Peach. It was a single-seater, and the outrigger tubes acted as exhaust pipes. Sliding pillar coil-spring front suspension was attached to cross-tubes which acted as a beam axle, and this inde-pendent set-up is similar to that used today. The trike's prop-shaft ran inside a central

13

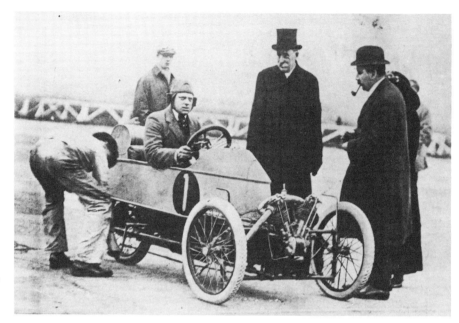

H. F. S. Morgan at Brooklands in November 1912, with his father wearing the top hat; a mechanic starts the engine as he embarks on his attempt on the one hour record. He travelled almost 60 miles in an hour, which was a considerable endeavour at the time, indicative of a sturdy and reliable machine. This photograph was used as the front cover of The Cyclecar *magazine dated 4 December 1912.*

backbone tube to the simple dog-and-sprocket two-speed transmission, which drove the back wheel with a chain on either side. Steering was by side-tiller, and foot and hand-operated rear-wheel braking was by a band on either side of the wheel.

The three-wheeler belonged to a particular species of motor vehicle called the cyclecar, and a Morgan was shown at the Earls Court Olympia Show in 1910. By 1911 the open three-wheeler had been clad in rudimentary bodywork and had two seats, and it was met with much acclaim; one of the first agencies for Morgan was Harrod's Store. The following year, the garage business was abandoned in favour of the increasingly profitable three-wheeler factory, and by 1914, production was running at 1,000 units a year. It goes without saying that Morgans have always been bought by sports-minded motorists; the superb power-to-weight ratio saw to that. HFS and owners including Harry Martin began competing at Brooklands, with HFS managing to achieve 60 miles (100 kilometres) in one hour in

November 1912. The following year W.G. McMinnies won the French cyclecar Grand Prix at Amiens, averaging 42mph (67km/h) over 163 miles (261 kilometres). Sixty years later, McMinnies challenged HFS's grandson Charles to a long distance race, to be held over 24 hours. The 88-year-old racer travelled by train and covered 1,200 miles (1,920 kilometres), whilst the young Morgan went by 4/4 and covered 1,320 miles (2,112 kilometres). Times change, but back in 1913, McMinnies' win in France prompted the introduction of a lightweight racing model known as the Grand Prix, which used the MAG engine.

One drawback to being in the cyclecar category was that Morgans had to run in the motorbike-and-sidecar class in certain events, since owners of four-wheelers refused to race against them. In everyday use, the main advantage of three-wheeler ownership was that at £4 a year, road tax was half that of a four-wheeler like an Austin Seven. Being light, at under 8cwt (400kg), the Morgan three-wheelers provided

70mph (112km/h) performance with 45mpg (6.3l/100km) economy. In general, three-wheelers were conceived by motorcyclists for use when marriage put an end to antics on two wheels, and the controls were more akin to those of a bike than a car. Even the 1930s Super Sports retained accelerator, choke and ignition-advance hand controls on the steering wheel. The engines too were invariably motorcycle V-twins.

Competition successes and the attendant publicity gained Morgan a strong reputation, and even then demand for 'cyclecars' exceeded supply. The Great War intervened, with the Morgan factory producing mainly shells, although other new models were developed at the same time, including a four-wheeler prototype in 1915, which is still in existence.

THE NEW FACTORY

In 1919, in a mood of post-war optimism, HFS acquired the Pickersleigh Road site,

and the whole operation was moved there in 1923, apart from the machine shop which transferred in 1929. A few hundred three-wheelers a year were produced under licence in France at the Courbevoie factory of Darmont et Badelogue, marketed as Darmonts. At Malvern, serious production began again in 1919, and a variety of different models and engine options was available. These were the halcyon days, as demand for personal transport was enormous, and Morgan reaped the proceeds. The 976cc Popular, which soon became the Standard, came with 8hp JAP or Blackburne engine, good for 75mph (120km/h), and cost £128 in 1923. The Grand Prix model was £155, and the MAG- or Anzani-engined 1,098cc Aero was slightly cheaper at £148. There was even a four-seater version, or perhaps two-plus-two would be more accurate, called the Family, with child seats either side of the rear wheel mudguard. This was also £148 with an air-cooled unit, or £158 for a water-cooled engine. A quick-release rear wheel was introduced, and a number of optional extras

Early days of the Pickersleigh Road factory, with Family models lined up in the dispatch bay, 1920.

15

Grand Prix three-wheelers under construction in the Pickersleigh Road factory in 1921; the radiator was an early fixture in the build process.

was available including electric lighting for an extra £8, with dynamo as standard from 1925; the Impirvo puncture-proof tyre fillings cost 7s 6d, or a four-speed gearbox was yours for £10.

The factory expanded as production increased, although there was a setback on the competition, and thus the publicity-generating, front. E. B. Ware's Morgan-JAP overturned in the 1924 Brooklands JCC 200-mile race and so upset were the organizers at the injuries sustained by the crew that all three-wheelers were banished to the ranks of motorcycles. Although three-wheelers could still take part in trials, it was not until the formation of the New Cyclecar Club in 1928 that three-wheelers could compete against cars again. But trials results were impressive in themselves. Morgans won no fewer than eleven gold and three silver medals in the MCC London to Edinburgh Trial in 1927.

Meanwhile, prices came down quite substantially as production increased, and competition grew tougher in the market-place. In 1926, there was a minimum two-week wait for delivery of a Morgan. Although

discounting is rife today, manufacturers never actually reduce their prices as happened in 1929 when the Family model could be bought for £87 10s, a drop of £60 in only six years. And models continued to evolve. By 1927, an electric starter was available for an extra £10, an electric horn could be ordered, certain models were equipped with front brakes, lubrication by grease-gun was introduced, and a more streamlined double-pane windscreen could be fitted. The Super Sports model came out at this time, costing £155 and powered by a high-compression ohv JAP engine. This engine could also be specified for the more spartan Aero model. In 1929, geared steering became standard, and sports models were equipped with wide track front suspension to improve stability. Gwenda Stewart achieved 115mph (184km/h) and set the kilometre class record at the Paris track of Montlhery the same year in a 998cc Super Sports JAP prepared by Douglas Hawkes. It was fuelled by undiluted alcohol, and at the end of her run, the tyres were virtually worn out. She returned to Montlhery the following year with S. C. H. Davis as co-driver to set more records.

The Morgan Runabout three-wheeler was in production during the 1920s; there were two models, Standard and Family. Here is a pristine example at the factory, admired by Peter Morgan's dog Jade.

Immaculate Matchless-engined 1933 Super Sports visits the factory. When racing at Brooklands the throttle was held wide open with elastic bands so the driver could use both hands to steer round the top of the banking.

From 1933 the F-series Family models were fitted with the four-cylinder 933cc Ford engine.

1,172cc side-valve engine mounted in a car-type chassis. There were a couple of stylistic innovations in the shape of a radiator and grille, and the Super Sports' spare wheel was housed in its barrel-shaped tail. The end of the line for the three-wheelers did not come until 1952, although very few were produced after 1946; just after the Second World War a batch of 990cc Matchless-engined trikes was shipped to Australia. There was thus a certain amount of overlap with the four-wheeler cars introduced in 1935. Sales of three-wheelers had begun to dip in the early 1930s, despite the price cuts, and exports were minimal due to less benevolent tax concessions abroad than those enjoyed in the UK; after the Second World War, steel was almost a precious metal, and supplies were allocated in the first instance to manufacturers exporting their products. Despite their new agencies abroad, Morgan found few takers for three-wheelers. So although the three-wheeler would always be his greatest thrill, HFS took the decision to conform to market forces with a sports car, whilst incorporating several of the Morgan's existing features such as the independent suspension and separate gearbox.

ENTER THE FOUR-WHEELER MORGAN

The first Morgan car was based on an F-type three-wheeler, and originally ran with a Ford 8 engine. It was called the 4–4, which stood for four wheels and four cylinders. These 4–4s, retrospectively known as Series I cars, were in production from 1936 to 1950, and curiously the numerology changed to 4/4 after the war. The first production 4–4s had roadster bodies, with removable hoods and sidescreens, and were powered by the 1,112cc Coventry Climax unit, which had overhead inlet and side exhaust valves.

In 1930 the original two-speed transmission gave way to a three-speed gearbox which was located at the end of the prop-shaft, driving the rear wheels by a single chain. It was still virtually motorcycle territory as far as the mechanicals went, with hand throttles and cable controls, and a three-wheeler was often the transitory phase between motorbike and car. If you could service your bike, you could cope with a Morgan.

As the small family car market increased, making ownership of a Ford Popular possible for £100, the F-type Morgan was introduced in 1933 to counter-attack with a Ford

4–4 Series I (1936–1939; called 4/4 1946–1950)

Layout and Chassis

Two- and four-seater sports and coupé models. Steel Z-section side-members with inverted U-shaped cross-members rivetted and welded: detachable frame-front

Engine

Type	Coventry Climax, Standard Special from 1939
Block material	Cast iron
Head material	Cast iron
Cylinders	4 in-line
Cooling	Water
Bore and stroke	Coventry Climax: 63 × 90mm
	Standard Special: 63 × 100mm
Capacity	Coventry Climax: 1,122cc
	Standard Special: 1,267cc
Main bearings	3
Valves	Coventry Climax: 8 side-valve
	Standard Special: 8 ohv
Compression ratio	6.8:1
Carburettor	Coventry Climax: Solex 30HBFG
	Standard Special: Solex 30FAI
Max. power (DIN)	Coventry Climax: 34bhp @ 4,500rpm
	Standard Special: 38.8bhp @ 4,500rpm
Fuel capacity	Two-seater and coupé: 11 gallons (50l)
	Four-seater: 10 gallons (45l)

Transmission

Clutch	Borg & Beck single dry plate cushion connected to the gearbox by a short torque tube
Gearbox	4-speed Meadowes to 1938, Moss thereafter
Ratios	Meadowes: 4th 5.0:1, 3rd 7.0:1, 2nd 12.0:1, 1st 17.5:1, Reverse 26.0:1
	Moss: 4th 5.0:1, 3rd 6.7:1, 2nd 11.95:1, 1st 19.3:1, Reverse 22.35:1

Suspension and steering

Front	Sliding stub axles on king pin, coil springs, and Newton dampers
Rear	5- and 6-leaf semi-elliptic springs, Hartford scissor-type friction dampers
Steering	Burman Douglas cam-and-peg; turning circle: 33ft (10m)
Tyres	Dunlop 4½ × 17in or 5 × 16in
Wheels	Coupé: 16in pressed steel; roadster: 17in Easiclean
Rim width	5in

Brakes

Type	Girling
Size	8in drums front and rear; 9in from 1949
	Fly-off handbrake

Dimensions (in/mm)

Track	
Front	45/1,143
Rear	45/1,143
Wheelbase	92/2,337
Overall length	140/3,556
Overall width	54/1,372
Overall height	Two-seater: 52/1,321; Four-seater: 54.5/1,384
Weight, full tank	Two-seater: 1,736lb/781kg; Four-seater: 1,792lb/806kg
	Coupé: 1,820lb/819kg

One of the first four-wheelers, this 1936 4–4 sets the general style for the first fifteen years of Morgan production. This example shows rounded 'droopy' front wings typical of the earlier cars, bar-mounted headlights, and 'flying M' mascot which screws into the radiator cap.

This 1936 Coventry Climax-engined 4–4 has a wire mesh stone guard over its radiator, carried over from the F-series Family three-wheeler; vertical slats would be used by 1938; cutaway wings expose sliding pillar suspension.

(This was not the same as the Coventry Climax single ohc 1,100cc FWA/E fire-pump engine which was adapted so successfully by Colin Chapman and John Cooper in the mid-1950s.) Gearboxes were initially by Meadowes, and later on Moss units were used. Performance figures were 34bhp at 4,500rpm, with a 70mph (112km/h) top speed, and the two-seater was priced at £185 18s 6d. Cars were produced under licence by Paris agent Stewart Sandford. A four-seater body was brought out in 1937, and a drophead coupé with folding hood, higher doorline and framed sliding glass windows, the following year. By 1939, Morgan had sold 883 4–4s, so they were obviously well received by the motoring public.

Back in 1937, 4–4s did well in the RAC Rally, and Miss Prudence Fawcett's entry in the 1938 Le Mans 24-hour race finished second in class and thirteenth overall, and fourteenth the following year. This spawned a handful of Le Mans replica models which featured fold-down windscreens and cycle-wing front mudguards. The engine of the Le Mans car had been underbored at the Coventry Climax factory so that it was eligible for the 1,100cc class, and the replicas, possibly five in number, followed suit. There was one, instead of two, spare wheel mounted on the rear panel. Works-backed Morgan activity in the Tourist Trophy event resulted in a small number of TT replicas, again probably six cars in total, also powered by the 1,098cc Climax engine. These were slightly less austere inside as outright speed was not the principal issue. By then supplies of the Triumph-built Coventry Climax engines were in jeopardy due to Triumph's financial problems, so HFS called on his friend Sir John Black at Standard to supply modified 1,267cc Standard Ten units.

During the Second World War, only the spares and service departments functioned. Part of the premises was leased to the

---

Avon Coupé

Finding himself in competition with MG in the late 1930s, HFS dispatched a chassis to Avon Motor Bodies to see what they would come up with to rival MG's drophead coupé. The result was an attractive flat-rad two-seater with full scuttle-height doors and metal spare wheel cover on its sloping rear deck. However, it proved too expensive to produce *en masse*, so Morgan went ahead with its own less curvaceous coupé in 1938. The Avon Coupé was used as a factory development car by works manager George Goodall, and subsequently fitted with a Standard Special engine. Owing to his habit of going trialling in it during the winter months, the car gained the whimsical appellation 'Uncle George's Winter Carriage'. The Avon Coupé is currently owned by Dave Rudge, Series 1 4–4 Registrar.

EB Morgan

In addition to the twenty-six Plus-4-Plus bodyshells styled and fabricated for Morgan by Tunstall-based Edwards Brothers Plastics, EB also made a single soft top two-seater in fibreglass. This was mounted on a 4/4 chassis using the Series V 4/4 powertrain and running gear. Known as the EB Morgan, it resides in the Netherlands and the Cortina unit has subsequently been replaced by a Ford Kent engine (see page 33).

Standard Motor Company and Flight Fuelling, who had a Handley Page Hereford bomber built in the wood shop. The machine shop was given over to making Spitfire undercarriage parts, breech-blocks for Oerlikon anti-aircraft guns and shell casings, and fortunately, when peace came in 1945, everything emerged unscathed. The Standard engine contract remained in place, and these engines were fitted as standard, as it were, and known as Standard Specials. Although HFS was tempted to manufacture his own engine at this time due to the difficulties of obtaining an appropriate power unit, Morgan was never to make its own engines. And this was the only engine to have the Morgan name embossed on the rocker cover. Individual engine builders were dropping out of the market at the time such as Maudsley, Meadows, and Anzani. HFS's son Peter Morgan, the current Chairman, recently described TVR's latest engine-building programme as 'highly precarious'.

However, when Triumph and Standard merged in 1945, the days of the 4/4 engine were numbered. Although the 1,267cc unit was dropped, HFS was reluctant to use anything larger than 1,500cc, mainly for the economical benefit of his customers, but a deal was arranged based on the Vanguard prototype being powered by a Continental-built 1,760cc engine. But when the Vanguard came out, the cubic capacity of its

---

Plus 4 (1950–1969)

Layout and Chassis
Two- and four-seater sports and drophead coupé, including fibreglass-bodied Plus-4-Plus and Super Sports competition models; Z-section side-members, welded box-section cross-members

Engine

Type	1950–1958: Vanguard
	1954–1969: Triumph TR2, 3, 3A, 4, 4A
Block material	Cast iron
Head material	Cast iron
Cylinders	4 in-line
Cooling	Water; Super Sports has oil cooler
Bore and stroke	Vanguard: 85 × 92mm
	TR2/3: 83 × 92mm
	TR4: 86 × 92mm
Capacity	Vanguard: 2,088cc
	TR2/3: 1,991cc
	TR4: 2,138cc
Valves	8 ohv
Compression ratio	Vanguard: 6.7:1
	TR2: 8.5:1
	Super Sports: 9:1
Carburettor	Vanguard: single Solex downdraught
	TR2: twin SUs
	TR3: twin SU R6
	TR4: Stromberg or SU
	Super Sports: Weber 42 or 45 DCOE
Max. power (DIN)	Vanguard: 68bhp @ 4,300rpm
	TR2: 98bhp @ 4,800rpm
	TR3: 100bhp @ 5,000rpm
	TR4A: 104bhp @ 4,700rpm
	Super Sports: 125bhp @ 5,500rpm
Fuel capacity	Two-seater and coupé: 11 gallons (50l)
	Four-seater: 10 gallons (45l)

Standard-built engine had risen to over 2.0-litres. Peter Morgan describes this as 'disastrous for a sports car, placing it amongst the 3.0-litre brigade at somewhere like Silverstone'.

THE FIRST PLUS 4

It was a case of take it or leave it, so here was the source for Morgan's new engines, and happily HFS was impressed by the level of torque. An appreciator if not a user of the automatic gearbox, he boasted of having driven from Maidenhead to Malvern using only top gear! Chassis modifications were necessary for the use of the 2,088cc former Ferguson tractor engine, and the model was known as the Plus 4. 'Plus' was a way of saying the model had more poke than the base model 4/4. It was announced at the 1950 Earls Court Show, and within a couple of years, a roadster, four-seater and drop-head coupé were available. A heater (or

Transmission

Clutch	Borg & Beck single dry plate cushion connected to the gearbox by a short torque tube
Gearbox	Moss 4-speed
Ratios	High: 4th 3.73, 3rd 4.5, 2nd 6.5, 1st 11.1:1
	Low: 4th 3.73, 3rd 5.2, 2nd 7.4, 1st 12.8:1
Final Drive	Salisbury: 4:1 or 3.73:1

Suspension and steering

Front	Sliding stub axles on king pin, coil springs, and Girling telescopic dampers
Rear	Semi-elliptic leaf springs with Girling or later Armstrong lever-arm dampers
Steering	Cam Gears cam-and-peg; turning circle: 33ft (10m)
Tyres	Dunlop 5.25 × 16in; 5.60/165-section from 1959
Wheels	16in disc; 15in disc or 60-spoke wires from 1959; 72-spoke wires from 1962
Rim width	5in

Brakes

Type	Girling drum; front discs optional from 1959, standard from 1960
Size	9in diameter drums front and rear; 11in discs

Dimensions (in/mm)

Track	
Front	47/1,194
Rear	47/1,194
Wheelbase	96/2,438
Overall length	140/3,556; from 1954: 149.25/3,791
Overall width	56/1,422
Overall height	50/1,270; from 1954: 54/1,372
Unladen weight	1,792lb/806kg

1951 Plus 4 drophead coupé taking part in the Welsh Rally, 12 July 1952.

fug-stirrer) was optional from this point. There had been something of a price-hike, since a pre-war 4/4 Le Mans Replica cost £250, and the Plus 4 was £625.

Although stylistically similar, the Plus 4 was actually a slightly larger car than the 4/4. The same differences between the three model options were carried over, so that the drophead coupé was a more grown-up car than the roadster; the hood was more versatile than the roadster, as it could be lowered completely or fixed halfway back. The drophead coupé's door-line was at the same height as the bonnet and rear wing, the windscreen could not be folded down, there were no louvres in the bonnet top, and no scuttle vent. But instead of being hand-painted, all cars were now sprayed with ICI cellulose.

Along with this major innovation came the first of a series of facelifts. Whereas the headlights and central dip or passing light had been attached to a badge bar ahead of the radiator grille, in 1953 the headlamps were incorporated into the front panel in tubes between wing and grille. Flashing indicators were optional from 1954. The

grille itself was now angled back more, and clad in a rounded cowl, and this is known as the interim-cowled stage, but is a rarity since only nineteen were made and possibly only two survive. With the revision of the rear spring location, and abandonment of the trunnion tube, there was nothing on which to fix the frame for supporting the spare wheels, so from 1955 a single spare was attached by studs to a bracket in a recess in the sloping rear deck; or in the case of the four-seater, in an upright position.

The transition to modern Morgan came in 1956 when the headlights were housed in teardrop-shaped fairings, and the inverted quarter-moon of the interim-cowl gave way to the fully slatted look, known as the 'high-cowl'. There would be one more significant change in Morgan body language, but not until 1966 when all Plus 4s got low-line bodies.

Meanwhile, at the 1951 Motor Show, Sir John Black asked Morgan if they would like to amalgamate to produce a sports car for the United States. HFS declined, and Peter Morgan recalls a sense of relief at this, preferring to concentrate on the British market. Triumph built the TR2 themselves, but this was always a heavier car than the Morgan. Morgan's success in competition was an aggravation to Triumph's Ken Richardson, and the supply of engines was mysteriously reduced from seven engines a week to four. This was the reason for the re-introduction of the 4/4, because Ford engines were more easily available.

ROAD TEST

Reproduced from *Motor*
19 September 1951

It has for many years past been the proud claim of the Morgan Motor Company that their cars were faster than anything else obtainable at the same price. Costing rather more than preceding models from the factory at Malvern, but also performing very much better than its predecessors, the latest 'Plus Four' Morgan proved on a recent 1,900-mile, 11-day road test that the 'fastest at the price' claim of its manufacturers remains very fully justified.

Sporting two-seater cars, built to a price limit which keeps them within reach of a large and reasonably youthful public, are an established part of Britain's range of car types. Emphasis on performance at a moder-ate price means that, inevitably, touring car luxury and carrying capacity are sacrificed to a greater or less extent. But, given acceptance of this bartering of spaciousness for speed, the open two-seater Morgan is a car which can give immense pleasure to the right sort of owner.

Effective Ingredients
The ingredients which go to make up the 'Plus Four' are simple and well known. An engine which propels the six-seater Standard Vanguard saloon (of 900 pounds greater unladen weight than the Morgan) at nearly 80mph, untuned save for elimination of any throttling by a carburettor silencer. A four-speed synchro-mesh gearbox which has already proved itself on sporting cars of much greater weight. A compact and low-built chassis, the layout and independent front-wheel suspension of which represent developments of previous Morgan designs. Finally, a body which is just the right size and shape for accommodating two people and a reasonable quantity of luggage.

The finished product, first and foremost, provides the outstanding performance on the road which is its raison d'etre. *It accelerates in an exhilarating manner which whisks it effortlessly past ordinary traffic, acceleration from a standstill to 50mph, for example tak-ing less than 10 seconds and 70mph being reached after only another 9.8 seconds. It also reaches usefully high maximum speeds when required, as witness the two-way mean speed of 84.7mph recorded, with hood and side-screens erected, during our performance tests in Belgium, but acceleration and hill climb-ing are the car's finest features. So far as a 'best' cruising speed can be defined, we would put it at a genuine 70–75mph for long or short journeys.*

Speed is of limited use on busy roads without the backing of powerful brakes, and whilst it was not possible to extend our test into Alpine territory it can safely be said that the Girling hydraulic brakes of the Morgan will meet all normal demands. They are given a good deal of work to do, but check the car with a squeal of tyres in response to moderate and well-graduated pedal press-ures, in a dead straight line save at a morn-ing's first application in wet weather, when a front brake sometimes proved liable to grab. For parking, there is a handbrake lever with the sports car 'fly-off' pattern ratchet, but the effectiveness and accessibility of this were not truly worthy of the car.

A vital contribution to the car's sporting character is made by the four-speed

Test Conditions

Mild, showery weather with strong cross wind.
Smooth concrete surface (Ostend–Ghent motor road, Belgium)
dry during acceleration tests. Standard grade Belgian pump
fuel.

Test Data

Acceleration Times on Two Upper Ratios

	Top	3rd
10–30mph	7.8secs	5.4secs
20–40mph	7.9secs	5.2secs
30–50mph	7.7secs	5.8secs
40–60mph	8.2secs	7.3secs
50–70mph	11.3secs	–
60–80mph	19.9secs	–

Acceleration Times Through Gears

0–30mph	4.0secs
0–40mph	6.5secs
0–50mph	9.9secs
0–60mph	14.1secs
0–70mph	19.7secs
0–80mph	33.2secs
Standing Quarter Mile	19.5secs

Fuel Consumption

34.0mpg at constant 30mph
32.5mpg at constant 40mph
29.5mpg at constant 50mph
27.5mpg at constant 60mph
24.0mpg at constant 70mph
20.0mpg at constant 80mph

Overall consumption for 461 miles,
driving fast, 18 gallons = 25.6mpg

Dimensions and Seating

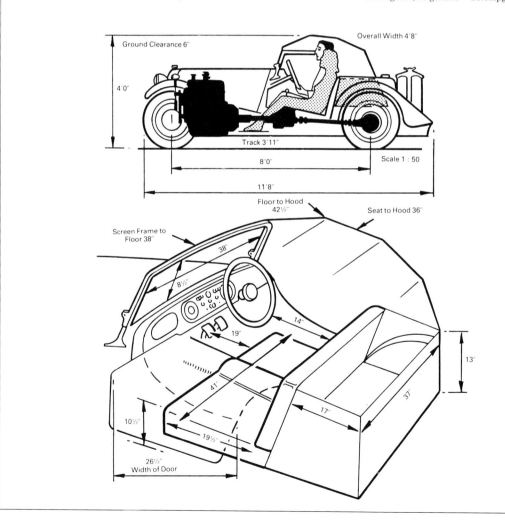

```
┌─────────────────────────────────────────────┐
│              Maximum Speeds                   │
│                                               │
│            Flying Quarter Mile                │
│ Mean of four opposite runs        84.7mph     │
│ Best time equals                  85.7mph     │
│                                               │
│               Speed in Gear                   │
│ Max speed in 3rd gear             68mph       │
│ Max speed in 2nd gear             47mph       │
│ Max speed in 1st gear             28mph       │
│                                               │
│ Weight                                        │
│ Unladen kerb weight               16cwt       │
│ Front/rear weight distribution    49/51       │
│ Weight laden as tested            19½cwt      │
│                                               │
│ Instruments                                   │
│ Speedometer at 30mph              2% slow     │
│ Speedometer at 60mph              3% fast     │
│ Speedometer at 80mph              4% fast     │
│ Distance recorder                 1% fast     │
│                                               │
│ Hill Climbing (At steady speeds)              │
│ Max top gear speed on 1 in 20     77mph       │
│ Max top gear speed on 1 in 15     72mph       │
│ Max top gear speed on 1 in 10     62mph       │
│ Max gradient on top gear  1 in 7.7 (Tapley 285lb/ton) │
│ Max gradient on 3rd gear  1 in 5.4 (Tapley 410lb/ton) │
│ Max gradient on 2nd gear  1 in 4 (Tapley 545lb/ton)   │
│                                               │
│ Brakes at 30mph                               │
│ 0.95g retardation (=31¾ft stopping distance) with 100lb │
│ pedal pressure                                │
│ 0.62g retardation (=48½ft stopping distance) with 75lb │
│ pedal pressure                                │
│ 0.37g retardation (=81ft stopping distance) with 50lb pedal │
│ pressure                                      │
│ 0.18g retardation (=167ft stopping distance) with 25lb │
│ pedal pressure                                │
└─────────────────────────────────────────────┘
```

synchro-mesh gearbox which, unusually, is located some distance behind the engine. The extremely short gear lever which projects from the top of the gearbox is ideally placed near to the steering-wheel rim, and although it is possible to beat the synchro-mesh, the change works excellently whether treated in a normal fashion or 'snatched' during some contest of speed. Giving very comfortable speeds of 20, 35 and 55mph, with much more in reserve if required, the gears are really useful for intensive motoring – although it should be emphasized that the engine retains normal touring flexibility right down to 10mph in top gear, and can take the car over quite astonishingly steep hills in that gear. The problems of insulating gearbox heat and

noise from the interior of the car seemed to have been quite adequately overcome on the test car, despite the unusual proximity of this unit to the driver.

Desirable Property

Given acceleration, speed and braking performances of a very desirable nature, the less easily defined qualities of general steadiness and controllability on the road are what really make a car desirable, acceptable or disappointing. Covering rather more than 500 miles in the Morgan during the first 24 hours after collecting it from the works, and another 1,400 before parting with it, those of our staff who drove and rode in the car were unanimous in putting it in the desirable category – this in spite of showery weather conditions which might have been thought ill-suited to open-car motoring, and of an appreciable number of points of detail criticism.

Essentially, the Morgan has the 'alive' character on the road which in an era of soft suspension and slow-to-respond steering is called 'old fashioned'. Considerably more flexibly sprung than its predecessors, and giving its passengers ample insulation against shock on any but the very worst surfaces, the chassis nevertheless does follow the contours of the road more precisely than do many of its contemporaries. In relation to the character of the car, of which reasonably firm springing is a natural part, our main criticisms of the suspension would be that the rear shock absorbers did not match the telescopic units fitted into the front suspension in ability to resist bouncing on awkward surfaces negotiated at high speed, and that at just 58mph there was a perceptible front-end shake on the test car. Our testing period in Belgium was unfortunately brief, but although the firmly sprung car was lively when rushed over pavée surfaces it did not give the impression that it would suffer from regular use on rough going.

Prompt Steering Response

The same 'alive' character which distinguishes the the car's riding is to be noted in the steering. There is no marked oversteering or understeering characteristic to attract comment, but rather a measure of balance, of prompt but not exaggerated response to steering wheel movements, which takes most of the conscious effort out of fast driving. There are imperfections; in the form of a rather unexpected springiness of the steering linkage which, feeling like slight lost motion, allow gusty side winds to induce wander of the car on straight roads; and in the form of castor action so progressive that considerable effort is needed to get full lock on a hair-pin corner. But, overall, the standard of easy controllability provided by the quick and reasonably reaction-free steering is very good.

Strictly sporting is the non-adjustable driving position, and for alert driving very comfortable also. The floor is the lowest part of the car, and although set well above floor level the driving seat also is very low, but there is a good forward view over the long bonnet. The way in which the floor is set low between the chassis side members means that entry to the car is not as easy as it might be, but once entered the cockpit is really comfortable, air-cushion seats giving support under the knees, and the backrest being upright and properly shaped. Instinctively, a driver feels a part of the car, and although a stranger is at first apt to find rather a lot of knobs and corners against which to bruise himself, consciousness of these is soon lost in appreciation of such details as rubber padding on top of doors cut away to form elbow rests of just the right height.

Luggage-carrying capacity is available in the back of the car, sufficient to meet the needs of most sports-car owners and protected from the elements by a tonneau cover, and there is also a glove compartment on the facia panel. For weather protection, two sidescreens which are easily mounted on the doors combine with the raked fold-flat windscreen to make the car very reasonably draught free – there is no trace of the common open car trouble of exhaust fumes sucked forwards into the cockpit. The hood is very weatherproof and not unduly slow to erect, a loose canvas panel (which can serve as a full-length tonneau cover if the car is parked) being secured by press-studs over a light-looking but apparently quite sufficiently strong folding frame.

Experience showed that a quite surprising amount of hood-down motoring was possible even in showery weather, since with the car in motion rain is thrown over the heads of the driver and passenger. Further, the presence of wide running boards as part of the car's effective mudguarding layout means that an elbow projecting through the flaps provided in the side-screens does not become wet as it does in so many low-built sporting cars. Owners of earlier types of Morgan will, incidentally, appreciate the considerably greater foot and elbow room made available by the new chassis.

Maintenance work would appear to be relatively simple on this car, the most vital parts of the sliding-pillar front suspension system having oil ducts from the engine and receiving lubrication when a pedal in the cockpit is pressed at recommended 100 mile intervals. Apart from being of simple design, the car gives easy accessibility to engine components.

Other running costs should be low in spite of the generous dimensions of the engine, high gear ratios and low car weight being valuable contributors to fuel economy. The figures for mileage per gallon quoted on our data page (25.6mpg overall) are creditable in themselves, but certain comparative interest attaches to results obtained on a 500-mile circuit of the Welsh mountains at fractionally over 30mph running average speed: with a ten-minute change-over of jets and choke

In Brief

Price, £535, plus purchase tax, £298 14s 6d equals
£833 14s 6d.

Capacity	2,088cc
Unladen kerb weight	16cwt
Fuel consumption	25.6mpg
Maximum speed	84.7mph
Maximum speed on 1 in 20 gradient	77mph
Maximum top gear gradient	1 in 7.7

Acceleration:

10–30mph in top	7.8secs
0–50mph through gears	9.9secs

Gearing:
18.4mph in top at 1,000rpm
76mph at 2,500ft per min piston speed

Specification

Engine

Cylinders	4
Bore	85mm
Stroke	92mm
Cubic capacity	2,088cc
Piston area	35.2sq in
Valves	Push-rod OHV
Compression ratio	6.7/1
Max power	68bhp
at	4,200rpm
Piston speed at max bhp	2,540ft per min
Carburettor	Solex downdraught
Ignition	Lucas oil
Sparking plugs	14mm Champion L10
Fuel pump	A.C Mechanical
Oil Filter	Fram

Transmission

Clutch	Borg & Beck s.d.p.
Gearbox	Set back behind engine
Top gear (s/m)	4.1
3rd gear (s/m)	5.4
2nd gear (s/m)	8.0
1st gear	13.5
Propellor shaft	Hardy Spicer, open
Final drive	Hypoid bevel

Chassis

Brakes	Girling, hydraulic, 21.s front
Brake drum diameter	9ins
Friction lining area	105sq in
Suspension: Front	Coil and slide IFS
Rear	Semi-elliptic
Shock absorbers: Front	Telescopic
Rear	Girling piston-type
Tyres	Dunlop 5.25-16

Steering

Steering gear	Burman
Turning circle	33 feet
Turns of steering wheel, lock to lock	2¼

Performance factors (at laden weight as tested)

Piston area, sq in per ton	36.1
Brake lining area, sq in per ton	108
Specific displacement, litres per ton mile	3,500

Fully described in 'The Motor,' October 18, 1950

Maintenance

Fuel tank: 11 gallons. **Sump:** 11 pints, SAE 30 Summer, SAE 20 Winter. **Gearbox:** 2½ pints., SAE 90 gear oil. **Rear axle:** 2½ pints SAE 90 hypoid oil. **Steering gear:** SAE 140 gear oil. **Radiator:** 11 pints (2 drain taps). **Chassis lubrication:** By grease gun every 1,000 miles to 3 points. Use steering lubricator pedal in cockpit every 100 miles. **Ignition timing:** Static 2° btdc. **Spark plug gap:** 0.32in. **Contact breaker gap:** 0.012in. **Valve timing:** IO, 10° btdc; IC, 50° abdc; EO, 50° bbdc; EC, 10° atdc. **Tappet clearances (cold):** Inlet, 0.010in, Exhaust 0.012in **Front wheel toe-in:** 0–⅛in. **Camber angle:** 2°. **Castor angle:** 4°. **Tyre pressures:** Front 18lb, Rear 18lb. **Brake fluid:** Girling crimson. **Battery:** 2 in series, 6-volt 57amp-hr. **Lamp bulbs:** 12-volt. Side and number plate, 6 watt, head 36/36 watt. Stop/tail 24/6 watt.

---

tube made before the start, at some very slight sacrifice of maximum speed but not seemingly of acceleration, and with a considerable amount of coasting indulged in, 36.8mpg was recorded in a long distance petrol consumption contest.

With either the normal carburettor settings used for obtaining the figures published on our data page, or the economy settings installed temporarily to suit a particular competition, the engine was unhesitating in response to the throttle almost immediately after it had been started from cold. The actual start from

cold was less immediate than on many cars which we test, but seemed entirely dependable and unaffected by overnight parking in exceptionally heavy rain.

Our overall impression of the Morgan is indicated by the fact of our running up more than double the conventional Road Test mileage during the modest period for which it was in our hands. It has short comings, but they do not seem terribly important when one is driving an open car, the vivacious character of which makes the use of it a potent rejuvenating tonic.

THE 4/4 RETURNS

Thus the 4/4 reappeared in 1955, powered by the side-valve 1,172 Ford Ten engine, and it was known as the Series II model. It was a fresh start for the 'entry-level' Morgan, as it was clad in the style of the high-cowl Plus 4, but being a smaller engine, the bonnet line was lowered and the body was altogether smaller than that of the Plus 4. In practical terms, this was manifest in an eight-gallon (36l) fuel tank, as opposed to the Plus 4's eleven gallons (50l). The link with Ford, now re-established, meant changing engines when stocks of the proprietary unit ran out, moving on to the subsequent engine. Many existing owners were quite happy to go along with this as well, since the 100E unit was only good for 76mph (122km/h) and traded up for the 997cc Anglia 105E unit which became available in 1960. This heralded the 4/4 Series III, which was quickly superseded the following year by the Series IV, which used the 1,340cc Classic engine. I had such an engine in my first car, an Anglia, in 1967, which (according to the speedo) could just do the ton! The competition version of the 4/4 used a single SU

4/4 Series II to V (1955–1968)

Layout and Chassis
Two-seater roadster; Z-section side-members, five welded box-section cross-members; detachable frame-front

Engine

Type	Ford 100E in Series II to 1960
	Anglia 105E in Series III to 1961
	Classic 109E in Series IV to 1963
	Cortina 116E in Series V to 1968
	Competition model fitted with Cortina GT unit
Block material	Cast iron
Head material	Cast iron; 1957 Competition model fitted with aluminium head
Cylinders	4 in-line
Cooling	Water
Bore and stroke	Series II: 63.5 × 92.5mm
	Series III: 80.97 × 48.41mm
	Series IV: 80.97 × 65.07mm
	Series V: 80.97 × 72.74mm
Capacity	Series II: 1,172cc; Series III: 997cc; Series IV: 1,340cc, Series V: 1,498cc
Valves	8; Series II: side-valve; Series III, IV & V: ohv
Compression ratio	Series II: 7:1; III: 8.5:1, IV & V: 8.3:1
Carburettor	Series II: Solex; Series III & IV: SU; Series V: Zenith, Weber (Competition model)
Max. power (DIN)	Series II: 36bhp @ 4,400rpm
	Series III: 39bhp @ 5,000rpm
	Series IV: 62bhp @ 5,000rpm
	Series V: 65bhp @ 4,800rpm
Fuel capacity	9 gallons (40l); 8.5 gallons (38l) from 1961

carburettor on a different manifold. The gearshift was on the Renault 4/2CV umbrella-handle principle, which must have been slightly ponderous in competition. The 1,340cc engine did not last long in the 4/4 though, being replaced with the Cortina's 1,498cc unit in 1963 and giving us the Series V. Wire wheels were offered on this model, and it used a Wooler remote gearshift and Armstrong Selectaride rear dampers. The Cortina GT engine with twin-choke Weber carb was available for competition use, and the final production Series V models of 1968 used the Lotus Cortina gearbox. The view of

the 4/4 at least during the 1950s was of a down-market model to make up the numbers. Production costs were naturally the same for a 4/4 as for a Plus 4.

Reverting to the Plus 4s, these carried on with the Vanguard engine from 1950 to 1958. The more sedate drophead coupé always had the Vanguard engine, but the roadster used the 90bhp TR2 engine from 1953. At 1,991cc, it was a Vanguard engine with twin SU carburettors, sleeved-down to allow cars to run in the under 2.0-litre classes. Here was the first production 100mph (160km/h) Morgan, and it could also

Transmission

Clutch	7½in diaphragm spring
Gearbox	Series II: Ford 3-speed;
	Series III, IV & V: Ford 4-speed; Wooler remote shift optional
Ratios	Series III & IV: 4th 4.56, 3rd 6, 2nd 11.1, 1st 18.8:1
Final Drive	Hardy Spicer prop-shaft to Salisbury 3HA hypoid bevel axle, 4.1:1 or 4.56:1

Suspension and Steering

Front	Sliding stub axles on king pin, coil springs, and Girling telescopic dampers
Rear	Semi-elliptic leaf springs with Armstrong lever-arm dampers; Selectarides optional on Series V
Steering	Cam Gears cam-and-peg; turning circle: 33ft (10m), or 31ft (9.4m) with 15in wheels
Tyres	5.20in, 5.25 × 16in; 5.60/165-section Dunlop C41 from 1959
Wheels	16in disc; 15in disc from 1960, or 60-spoke wires from 1963
Rim width	5in

Brakes

Type	Drum; umbrella-handle type handbrake until Series V fly-off type
Size	9in diameter drums front and rear; 11in diameter front from 1961

Dimensions (in/mm)

Track	
Front	47/1,194
Rear	47/1,194; Series V: 49/1,245
Wheelbase	96/2,438
Overall length	144/3,658
Overall width	56/1,422
Overall height	50/1,270
Unladen weight	Series II to IV: 1,456lb/655kg; Series V: 1,848lb/832kg

Wooden dashboard of a Series 1 1936 Morgan 4–4, with white-on-black instruments; wiper motor is above the scuttle, with drive shaft protruding through the screen.

Dash has metamorphosed through several changes to the style fitted in this 1982 4/4 with aero-screens. By this time all dashes were covered to match the interior trim.

make 0–60mph (0–96km/h) in ten seconds. The TR2 engine was available until 1957, and overlapped with TR3 units which had come on stream in 1955. The main difference between the two was the TR3's bigger SUs and a modified inlet manifold. The TR3 unit continued to be available for competition-minded owners after the larger-bore TR4 engine became standard. From 1962, the 2,138cc engine powered the Plus 4, and standardized to Stromberg carbs from 1965.

A couple of interesting variants bore the Plus 4 badge. These were the luxurious four-seater coupés, which had luggage boots with bottom-hinged lids covering the spare wheel, and wide, full-height rear-hinged doors. HFS drove one of these elegant cars, which originally had flat rads, changing to cowls from 1954. UK versions had the Vanguard engine, but those exported were fitted with TR2 units; only fifty-one were made, between 1951 and 1956. There was also a one-off saloon, built for a customer by Cooper Motor Bodies of Putney in 1952, based on a Plus 4 flat-rad chassis, and the car survives in restored condition in California.

LE MANS SUCCESS AND THE SUPER SPORTS

Peter Morgan took over the company reins when HFS died in 1959, sadly without seeing one of his cars win its class at the 1962 Le Mans 24-hour race. The entry was rejected in 1961 by the unpredictable and occasionally xenophobic scrutineers, who said it did not look like a modern sports racer; this despite the fact that it was a contemporary Plus 4. The man who drove it, Chris Lawrence, believes the real reason for the rejection was that the works Triumph team threatened to pull out of the race if they had to compete with their 'Sabrina' twin-cam engines against the Morgan's

production TR3 engine. The entry for an identical Super Sports, now fully backed by the factory, was accepted the following year. In the hands of Chris Lawrence and Giulietta racer Richard Shepherd-Barron, it finished thirteen out of eighteen cars still running at the end, and won the 2.0-litre GT class. The production Plus 4 Super Sports was a particularly special car, evolving directly from Lawrence's TOC 258. Instead of the contemporary Plus 4 bodies, which were still taller in 1962, the Super Sports copied Lawrence's car and were fitted with aluminium panelled 4/4 bodies. The TR3 or TR4 engines were sent away and stripped down at Lawrencetune in Acton, west London, where high-lift cams were fitted and the heads polished and gas-flowed. Other internals such as clutch, crank and flywheel were balanced at Jack Brabham Motors, and the ensemble was completed by a four-branch manifold and lusty 42- or 45-DCOE Weber carbs. To accommodate the inlet trumpets, a scoop had to be incorporated into the side of the bonnet, and the louvres ran the opposite way to those on the bonnet itself. Because of the lower cowl, the radiator had to be made shorter and thus needed a header tank. Of further significance was that the Super Sports' low-line body set the standard very firmly for the profile of future Morgans. Just 101 were made between 1962 and 1968, although the Lawrencetune conversion remained popular with owners of regular Plus 4s.

A CHANGE OF SHAPE: THE PLUS 4 PLUS

By the mid-1960s, Morgan sales in Europe and the UK were virtually at a standstill. In 1964, 83 per cent of production went to the States, but by 1968, the company was out of the American market altogether. In Europe, sales of Morgans were in the doldrums and it looked as if the cars were just not wanted any more. The early sixties was a period of recession in the States, and suddenly the market dropped, with orders in production, cars on the water, cars at the docks, and unsold in showrooms.

As a way of hurdling the stagnation and maintaining the company's market share, Peter Morgan decided to come bang up to date and introduce a new model. The fibreglass-bodied Plus 4 Plus came out at the 1963 Earls Court Motor Show, and despite its wonderfully curvaceous coupé lines built on the Plus 4 platform, it was rather snubbed by Morgan *aficionados*, who criticized its appearance as being too much like a Lotus Elite or Jaguar XK. Of course it is much coveted now, although Peter says he should have got the windscreen further forward to improve the shape. The Plus 4 Plus was built on a standard Plus 4 chassis, using the normal TR4 engine, and the extremely elegant body was by EB Plastics of Tunstall, Staffs. Being fibreglass, it was light and very fast, capable of 110mph (176km/h). But in the event, only twenty-six were built. It seemed customers wanted their Morgans to look like they had always done.

So it was that the 4/4 carried on using Ford engines, with the 1600 'Kent' Cortina Mark II engine coming in from 1968, when it was called the 4/4 1600. The Plus 4 used the TR4A engine until 1969, when Triumph went to six cylinders. The in-line six was too long for the Morgan, and in any case the Plus 8 was in the offing, and the Plus 4 was dropped until 1985.

ROAD TEST
Reproduced from *Motor Sport*
May 1963

All the other cars dealt with in this series of road tests of under £700 sports cars are in the

1,100cc category but the Morgan 4/4 is available with the 1,340cc or 1,500cc Ford Classic engines, giving the Morgan the best performance of the cars tested in this series and the worst fuel consumption, a fact of motoring life which seems inescapable.

With the 1,340cc engine the Morgan 4/4 is known as the Mk IV and costs a total of £659 2s 1d with the engine in standard form. With the 1½-litre engine and all-synchromesh gearbox it is known as the Mk V and costs a total of £683 5s 5d, once again with the engine in standard form. The car submitted to us for test was in actual fact the Competition version of the Mk IV which uses a single SU carburettor on a new inlet manifold in conjunction with a 4-branch exhaust manifold. Production cars of this type also have a rev-counter but the test car was not so fitted. With these modifications the price of the test car came over our £700 limit, working out at £731 12s 1d. The standard models will of course be slower and have better fuel consumption.

There is not a lot which can be said about the Morgan which has not already been said many, many times, as, apart from engine and gearbox variations, the design changes very little over the years, only slight body changes serving to distinguish the present model from its pre-war counterparts. The chassis has two deep Z-shaped side-members with five bracing cross-members, the front suspension is the same sliding pillar type patented by Morgan 40 years ago except that longer coil-springs are used, the rigid rear axle runs above the chassis side-members and is sprung on semi-elliptic leaf-springs, but a concession to modern trends is shown in the braking system, which uses 11in Girling discs on the front wheels and 9in drums at the rear.

There is little comparison between the Morgan and the other cars in this series as the others have been developed to the extent where they can be considered as completely weatherproof, comfortable touring cars with most of the amenities of comparable saloon cars, but the Morgan stays determinedly rugged and spartan, with few of the refinements which most modern sports car drivers demand. Getting in and out is a problem as the cut-away doors are narrow, the door sill is high, and the end of the scuttle provides a pointed edge to impale kneecaps with great accuracy. There are no external door handles so it is necessary to lift the flaps on the detachable sidescreens to reach inside and open the doors. However, as the flaps button down to keep out the rain it is sometimes necessary to bend the metal framework of the sidescreen to gain access unless you detach the sidescreen in its entirety, which is simple enough as the knurled knobs are on the outside. Once inside driver and passenger sit on upholstered cushions loosely placed on wedge-shaped wooden boxes which have no method of adjustment, and they lean against a one-piece back-rest which is also not adjustable. The driver is confronted by a huge 17in Bluemels 4-spoke steering wheel which is too large for the cramped conditions of the cockpit, as well as rubbing the driver's trousers. The brake and throttle pedals are well placed in relation to each other for the heel-and-toe changes but due to the wide gearbox tunnel there is no room to rest the left foot, which makes things difficult, especially as the Morgan handbook implores the owner (in large capitals) not to rest his foot on the pedal. The dipswitch is placed above the clutch pedal on the bulkhead and the plunger for front suspension oiling is above the gearbox tunnel. This plunger diverts engine oil to the sliding axles and should be pressed every 200 miles or so, although there is a childish tendency to do it more often, just to see the drop in oil pressure on the gauge. However, this can soon empty the sump, so is not really recommended.

The wooden dashboard follows normal Morgan practice with two cream-coloured instruments placed either side of the steering column, that on the right being a rather erratic Smiths 90mph speedometer with trip and total odometer, and the other one containing fuel contents, ammeter and oil-pressure gauges. A horn button is placed on the outer edge of the dashboard to the driver's right and in the centre is a batch of toggle switches in a separate panel which cover the operation of the panel lights, fog and spot-lamps (although the test car only had a spot fitted), direction indicators, and windscreen wipers. Pull-out knobs operate the choke and headlamps, a tiny press-button works the electric windscreen washers, and starting is by the ignition key. Warning lights in this panel show when the headlamp main beam is in operation, when the dynamo is not charging and when the flashing indicators are working. A 2-pin socket for an inspection lamp is also fitted in the centre panel.

In front of the passenger is an unlidded cubby-hole, which, with the space behind the seats, forms the only luggage accommodation in the car. To the left of the locker is the knob for the Smiths recirculatory heater which is fitted to the bulkhead. Of the items mentioned, the heater, spot-lamp and windscreen washer are all extras, costing £15 4s 6d, £8 12s 2d and £4 16s 1d, respectively, the price for the spot-lamp including the badge bar on which it is mounted. There is also a vast range of other extras (some of which many people might consider as essentials), such as wire wheels, leather upholstery, rear bumper, tonneau cover, wooden steering wheel, seat belts, luggage carriers, etc.

Having accustomed oneself to the cramped driving quarters of the Morgan it is quite refreshing to peer along a proper bonnet once more, with separate wings showing just where to point the car. Visibility is good through the flat screen but side and rear vision is rather restricted and the tiny rear-view mirror is inadequate.

Morgan have not adopted a proper remote-

35

control arrangement for the gear-lever but have fitted a push-pull lever like that used on the older 4/4 model and such cars as the 2CV Citroën and Renault 4. This takes some getting used to and although satisfactory changes can be made, the box is nowhere near as pleasant as that on the Ford from which the gearbox is taken. It is difficult to judge distances across the gate and we confess to hitting 1st occasionally when going from 2nd to 3rd, while we found reverse difficult to locate. However, we soon became accustomed to the peculiarities of this lever without coming to like it much. Clutch pedal pressure is light so that reasonably fast shifts can be made with determination.

The Morgan weighs in at around 13cwt dry so the Ford engine endowed it with fairly brisk acceleration, which places it ahead of the other cars tested in this series as far as performance goes. It is relatively noisy in the Morgan, setting up a sympathetic vibration somewhere in the car when approaching peak revs, but it will pass through this period and smooth out until valve bounce is reached. The gearbox is not unduly noisy and the main source of noise at speed comes from colossal wind roar around the windscreen pillars, which is also the source of numerous draughts inside the car which become a little too uncomfortable in really cold weather. Fortunately with the heater fan switched on at full blast the heat just about counterbalances the incoming draughts. Another fault found on the test car was its lack of weather protection, the screen becoming almost as wet on the inside as on the outside in heavy rain, and as there are no such refinements as demisting slots on the scuttle a plentiful supply of clean rag is necessary to keep the screen clear on the inside.

The ride of the Morgan is softer than previous Morgans we have tried due to the longer coil-springs, but it still has about the harshest ride of any current production sports car. On smooth main roads the ride is quite acceptable, small bumps not being particularly noticeable, but as soon as any serious undulations are crossed the suspension bottoms viciously, lifting the occupants out of their seats and dropping them back with a spine-jarring crash. There is also some scuttle shake under these conditions, a problem which is nearly always present in cars of this type of construction. The harshness of the suspension spoils high-speed driving for most people as it is necessary to reduce speed drastically when running on bad roads. On smooth roads the 4/4 will cruise quite happily at an indicated 80mph, although with its 4.56:1 axle ratio the engine sounds quite busy. It should be possible to fit the 4.1:1 ratio of the Classic for quieter cruising in the higher speed ranges. On the present ratio the car will reach speeds of 27, 45, 65 and 90mph in the gears, but engine rpm is near 6,000rpm at maximum speed. Acceleration from rest to 60mph in 13.7sec is some 2sec better than the Spitfire and 2.7sec better than the Midget, while it shows an even greater improvement to 70mph with a time of 17.4sec, which is 4.3sec faster than the Spitfire and 5.6sec faster than the Midget. It must be remembered, however, that the Morgan is the more expensive competition model.

The actual performance figures, with the best run in brackets, are shown below.

0–30mph	3.5sec	(3.1sec)
0–40mph	6.2sec	(6.0sec)
0–50mph	10.2sec	(10.0sec)
0–60mph	13.7sec	(13.4sec)
0–70mph	17.4sec	(17.0sec)
s.s.¼-mile	19.0sec	(18.9sec)

On smooth bends the Morgan handles particularly well as the taut suspension allows little roll, and it is possible to make the C41 Dunlops squeal heavily without inducing breakaway on dry roads. On bumpy corners axle hop is experienced and the driver is given the feeling that the front and rear

MORGAN 4/4 SERIES IV

Engine: *Four cylinders, 80.96 × 65.07mm (1,340cc). Push-rod-operated overhead valves. 8.5:1 compression ratio. 56.5bhp at 5,000rpm*
Gear ratios: *1st, 18.8 to 1; 2nd, 11:1; 3rd 6:1; top, 4.56:1*
Tyres: *5.60 × 15in Dunlop C41 on bolt-on disc wheels*
Weight: *13cwt (dry)*
Steering ratio: *2¼ turns lock-to-lock*
Fuel capacity: *8½ gallons. (Range approximately 230 miles)*
Wheelbase: *8ft*
Track: *Front, 3ft 11in; rear, 3ft 11in*
Dimensions: *12ft × 4ft 8in × 4ft 4in (high)*
Price: *£545 (£659 2s 1d with purchase tax). Competition model as tested £760 4s 10d*
Makers: *Morgan Motors Ltd, Pickersleigh Road, Malvern Link, Worcestershire.*

brought the car to the notice of a much larger public due to their numerous competition victories. The fact remains that the present-day sports-car buyer demands a far higher degree of comfort and habitability than the Morgan offers. Compared with its competitors in the under-£700 class the 4/4 has less interior room, less luggage space, a much firmer ride and a general lack of refinement and detail finish, while many buyers in this price class may feel that a petrol thirst of 28.5mpg, which is what we obtained, is too much compared with the 33.7mpg on the Spitfire and 39.2mpg of the MG Midget.

M.L.T.

ENTER THE PLUS 8

The 1960s was a lean decade for Morgan, because of the obsession with the new and trendy. Britain, in particular, had finally broken free of post-war austerity, and the accent was on youth, outrage, frivolity and freedom, even if these were bogus unattainable states. The downside was that anything traditional and smacking of the past was debunked, kitsched-up or scoffed-at. Vehicles like the Mini Cooper, E-type and Elan were flash and fashionable and the Morgan was not. Despite a loyal die-hard following, boosted by the class win at Le Mans, this was reflected in desperately poor sales. Cars were displayed by agents on a sale or return basis, and for instance if a car had not sold in four or five weeks, agents such as Bolton's of Leeds or Basil Roy in London's Great Portland Street sent it back to be swapped for a different coloured model; people would assume the departed car had been sold and think things were not quite so bad. It was a far cry from the waiting list which grew in the early seventies. In addition, there were problems with US legislation in 1966, which stopped Morgan from exporting cars to the States. Rover saw Morgan as ripe for a

suspensions are out of phase, the front end dancing about noticeably while the tail sits down fairly happily. The steering is reasonably light and with only 2¼ turns lock-to-lock corrections are easily made, but a smaller steering wheel and more elbow room in the cockpit would give the driver more confidence as he sits in a rather hunched-up position.

The brakes are smooth, powerful and progressive, and stop the car well under all circumstances with no sign of fade or grab. However, the umbrella-type handbrake fitted under the dashboard is completely out of character with this type of car although working reasonably well.

It seems incredible that a car which has changed only in small details, apart from various different engines, since well before the war is still selling at all, but the small factory is still quite busy sending cars all over the world. Much of the credit for this must go to Chris Lawrence and Richard Shepherd-Barron, whose exploits with the Lawrencetune Morgan Super Sports have

Plus 8 (1968–1990)

Layout & Chassis
Two-seater sports; deep Z-shape section with five boxed or tubular cross-members; detachable frame-front

Engine

Block material	Aluminium alloy
Head material	Aluminium alloy
Cylinders	90° V8
Cooling	Water; Wood Jefferies auxiliary electric fan
Bore and stroke	88.90 × 71.12mm
Capacity	3,528cc
Main bearings	5
Valves	16
Compression ratio	1968: 10.5:1; Rover P6/3500 engine
	1973: 9.35:1; high-octane fuel becomes unavailable
	1976: 9.25:1; Rover SD1 engine
	1984: 9.75:1; SD1 Vitesse engine
Carburettors	1968: Twin SU HS6
	1973: SU H1 F6
	1981: Stromberg
	1984: Lucas electronic fuel-injection
Max. power (DIN)	1968: 151bhp @ 5,000rpm
	1973: 143bhp @ 5,000rpm
	1976: 155bhp @ 5,000rpm
	1984: 190bhp @ 5,280rpm
Max. torque	1968: 210lb/ft @ 2,750rpm
	1973: 202lb/ft @ 2,700rpm
	1984: 220lb/ft @ 4,000rpm
Fuel capacity	13.5 gallons (61l)

Transmission

Clutch	Single plate diaphragm spring
Gearbox	Moss 4-speed with torque tube (first 484 cars)
	4-speed Rover from 1972 (702 cars)
	5-speed Rover from 1976
Ratios	Moss: 4th 3.73, 3rd 5.2, 2nd 7.4, 1st 12.8:1
	Rover: 4th 1.0, 3rd 1.391, 2nd 2.133, 1st 3.625:1
	Rover: 5th 0.79, 4th 1.0, 3rd, 1.39, 2nd 2.08, 1st 3.32:1; Reverse 3.42:1
Final Drive	Salisbury 7HA hypoid bevel axle. Powr-Lok limited-slip differential; ratio 3.58:1 , 3.31:1 from 1973

takeover bid at this point, but the tentative offer was rejected.

What came out of the discussions was the offer of Rover's new, light all-aluminium alloy 3.5-litre V8 power unit, derived from the excellent but redundant Buick engine. Thus the Morgan took another quantum leap in 1967 when the Maurice Owen-developed prototype Plus 8 first turned a wheel. This was actually a modified Buick unit rather than a proper Rover engine, so modest bonnet bulges were necessary to house the SU carburettors mounted on the American manifold. After supply problems

Suspension and Steering

Front	Independent by vertical coil springs on sliding stub axle; Armstrong telescopic dampers
Rear	5 semi-elliptic leaf springs (a few have 6); Armstrong lever-arm dampers
Steering	AC Delco extruded mesh collapsible column, Cam Gears cam-and-peg type to 1986, turning circle: 40ft (12.2m); thereafter Jack Knight rack-and-pinion, turning circle 38ft (11.6m)
Wheels	15in cast alloy, five-stud 14in Millrace from 1977 15in magnesium alloy from 1982
Tyres	Dunlop SP Sport 185VR15; Dunlop SP195VR14; Pirelli P6, Avon or Uniroyal 205/60VR15
Rim width	5½in, 6in, 6½in

Brakes

Type	Girling hydraulic dual-circuit, with servo to October 1981; fly-off handbrake
Size	11in diameter discs front; 9 × 1.75in drums rear

Dimensions (in/mm)

Track	
Front	1968: 49/1,245 1973: 51/1,295 1976: 53/1,346
Rear	1968: 51/1,295 1973: 52/1,321 1976: 54/1,372
Wheelbase	1968: 96/2,438 1969: 98/2,489
Overall length	1968: 152/3,861 1976: 156/3,962
Overall width	1968: 57/1,448 1973: 59/1,499 1976: 62/1,575 1983: 63/1,600
Overall height	1968: 50/1,270 1976: 48/1,219
Unladen weight	1968: 1,900lb/855kg 1973: 1,884lb/848kg 1976: 2,068lb/931kg

during the Leyland takeover of Rover had been overcome, which included the red herring offer to Morgan of the Triumph Stag's V8 engine, the Rover V8-engined Plus 8 made it to Earls Court in 1968, and was available for testing by *Autocar* in September 1968. Performance figures were exactly what was required to boost the image: 0–60mph (0–96km/h) in 6.7 seconds, and a maximum of 124mph (198km/h). Here was something to get on terms with the flashy speed merchants of the day. Around this time, Morgan's fortunes started to pick up again; customers began to perceive that the

Front suspension layout of Plus 8, showing coil springs and rack-and-pinion steering.

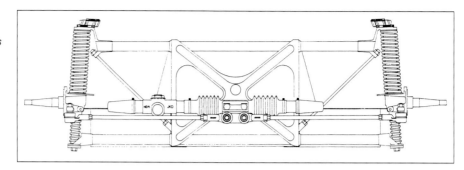

The semi-elliptical rear springs of the Plus 8.

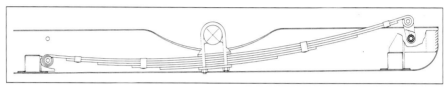

Morgan was a car that stood out from the crowd, although Britain was the last market to get going. Agents in Germany and France had considerable success.

The Rover V8 engine was not homologated in the United States until 1970, so Morgan did not get back into the US market until 1971. It was a short-lived return because the Rover 3500 saloon was not a hit there, and the company pulled out. Because Morgan was using the Rover engine, the Plus 8 would have been required to complete a constant-running 50,000-mile (80,000-kilometre) test in order to remain on sale in the USA. This was an incredibly boring task, because there were no dynamometers or rolling roads then. Morgan had previously completed a 3,000-mile (4,800-kilometre) run for small manufacturers on a 45-mile (72-kilometre) lap around Coventry, but declined to pursue the matter. From the mid-1970s US agent Bill Fink at Isis Imports, San Francisco, converted the Plus 8 to run on propane, and it has been like that ever since. In turbocharged form, it could still do 128mph (205km/h) and 0–60mph (0–96km/h) in 6.8 seconds. The company has recently managed to obtain Federal approval

for a petrol-consuming V8, but there have always had to be compromises on safety aspects, particularly problematic in California. The low-speed telescopic bumper is in use, side-impact bars are now installed, even sun visors, and the next hurdle is airbags. Morgan is working with a Breed unit. Nevertheless, Peter Morgan believes the US market can never return to what it was in the fifties for a small manufacturer, because of the difficulty a small manufacturer has in keeping up to date with safety requirements. Potentially ruinous public liability claims also conspire to make it not worth Morgan's while. In the event, most of the volumes formerly sold in the United States have been taken up elsewhere in other foreign markets, notably Europe, Australia and Japan.

The Plus 8 has only ever been marketed as a roadster, although one four-seater was made and sold to agent Eric White at Cranfield. There may be others; that of the celebrated disc jockey John Peel, an early Plus 8, was in the process of being converted to a four-seater when I visited the factory. (And whilst we're name-dropping, other Morgan showbiz owners have included Mick Jagger,

Brigitte Bardot and Peter Sellers.) A drophead coupé was also produced, but the folding hood mechanism was judged to be too uneconomical to make *en masse*. This particular car is owned by Mrs Jane Morgan, and it runs with Rover 3500 automatic transmission, making it a unique car in two senses. The 3,528cc 3.5/P6 engine was fed by twin SU carbs, and used an alternator instead of the customary dynamo. To accommodate this, the offside front wing was cut away, and the nearside was trimmed to match. Emissions restrictions brought about a lower compression ratio which emasculated power output to 143bhp. However, the SD1's updated 3500 unit introduced in 1976 restored output to a more respectable 155bhp. The engine position was shifted backwards, and the post-1976 square-section rocker covers and carb set-up (Strombergs from 1981) used a smaller air filter which was clear of the bonnet hinge; previously it had been necessary to resort to prehistoric techniques involving a hammer and a block of wood to dent the top of the air filter to get it under the bonnet. With the SD1 Vitesse model of 1983 came fuel injection instead of the twin SU carburettors, but the snag now involved the injection's plenum chamber. A sliver was cut from the bonnet hinge itself. This engine benefited from improved porting and a higher compression ratio, delivering a decent 190bhp at 5,280rpm. Acceleration was down to 5.6 seconds for the 0–60mph (0–96km/h) sprint, but it was felt by some that it was the Morgan's pre-war aerodynamics that restricted its top speed to 122mph (195km/h).

With the demise of the V8-engined Auntie Rover saloons, the most recent engine change involved fitting the Land Rover-built Range Rover 3,946cc V8 in 1990. The addition of an optional catalytic converter, originally developed for the German market, had little effect on the Plus 8's performance, and in fact torque improved. The 12-gallon (54l) fuel tank (14 gallons [63l] before 1990) was mounted on a deal board after 1986, having been previously supported on steel plates.

ROAD TEST

Reproduced from *Road & Track*
August 1980

Morgan Plus 8 Turbo

The year 1936 was a momentous one in Great

Britain: she had three sovereigns that year, with King George V dying in January, Edward VIII abdicating to marry the woman he loved, and his brother becoming George VI before year's end. In the midst of all this, one of her motorcar manufacturers, Morgan Motor Company Ltd, Malvern Link, Worcestershire, introduced its 4/4 model (that is, four each of cylinders and wheels) characteristically understating the point that 4-wheeled motoring might not be just something of a fad. To cover its bets, though, Morgan kept its 3-wheelers in production almost to the end of George VI's reign, 1950 to be exact. Beg pardon, ma'am; that's the Moggie Trike, not George VI.

And if you're wondering why, in this twenty-eighth year of Elizabeth II's reign, we're making such a big deal of things that happened so long ago, you've not reached the proper frame of mind for appreciating the subject of this road test, the Morgan +8 Turbo. In our '10 Best Cars for a Changed World,' R&T, June 1978, the Morgan garnered the coveted Henry N. Manney III Intransigence Can Be a Virtue Award. 'After all,' we noted 'if the basic design was good enough in the Thirties, it's surely adequate today.' And prior to that, our last Moggie road test was back in December 1969, so you can see that the long view is important. Why this thoroughly delightful car evaded our road test scrutiny for the entire decade of the Seventies is partly that very little new happened to the Morgan, partly simple economics and partly a good dose of Gummint. For a long time, Morgan has had waiting lists that would be the envy of any other automaker. And Pete Estes, Henry Ford and Lee Iacocca know what we're hinting at – you get to a point where there are just so many cars you care to make, and that's it. Complicated matters with piles of paper required to show the car is safe and sanitized, and you eventually come to think the US market is more trouble than it's really worth. As did Morgan in the early seventies.

Enter Bill Fink and his Isis Imports, Ltd, Inc, and US Morgan aficionados had cause for rejoicing. Bill set out single-handedly to import and legalize the marque, and his offerings today, both 4- and 8-cylinder models, are absolutely charming blends of old and new. And when we say old, we're not simply talking about last year's chrome trim being carryover.

Let's start at the front end by noting that Morgan's sliding-pillar independent suspension hasn't changed radically since the good H. F. S. Morgan set pen to drawing board in 1910. (Curiously enough, that's the year George V ascended the throne. See how much history we're learning?) In any case, the Morgan front suspension has steel tubes supporting two vertical pillars on which slide the hub/stub axle assemblies suspended by coil springs; disc brakes, hydraulic tube shocks and an optional decambering by Bill bring things more or less up to date. The rear suspension is a bit more modern, but then you've got to recall that the Morgan had only one wheel back there for the first 26 years. A live axle with Salisbury limited slip is suspended in semi-elliptic leaf springs and damped by lever-action shocks, those marvellous box-like contraptions whose sealing characteristics were always hinted at by the presence of little refill plugs.

These components attach to what is actually half the real suspending medium, a steel ladder frame of perhaps less than state-of-the-art rigidity. The tyres are the other half of the suspension: think of the springs as merely something to grease occasionally. An ash framework is assembled atop the ladder chassis, and this in turn is cloaked in steel panels (or, as is the case with our test car, several of optional aluminium alloy). Neat, effective and, as we noted as recently as 1969, if it was good enough for the Thirties, why not today? Well, in fact, the feds have stomped in since then, and Bill responds *with some added structure to fit the required door anti-intrusion beams. There's a hoop of rollbar stock behind the dash to which the door hinges are attached, another structure behind the cockpit on which the door latch posts reside, and Bill carves out a bit of ash door-frame to mount aluminium beams. Little of this shows, of course, but you can still see a painted edge of ash here and there, as is quite proper after all.*

Bill handles the fed's dodgem bumper regs cleverly, with hydraulic pistons taken from the Volkswagen Rabbit and attached to steel tubes backing up the stock Morgan bumpers. These and the relocated taillights look considerably less out of place than several factory botch-ups that come to mind.

Under the bonnet comes the real news since our last road test of a Morgan: The Isis/ Jaguar Rover Triumph/nee Buick V-8 is now propane-fueled and turbocharged. The first is a standard feature of Bill's 25-per-year output: the turbo installation is a $2500 option for those desiring added kick to their nostalgia. The switch to liquid petroleum gas (propane or butane) makes particularly good sense for a couple of reasons. First, it allows a complete lack of emission controls and the attendant problems with certification, durability testing and the like, what with LPG running as clean as Joan Claybrook escaping a Detroit steam bath. As an added benefit, propane's 105 octane means the 9.4:1 compression ratio is perfectly compatible with the Rajay turbo's 6-psi boost. There's no need for water injection or other detonation protection, and Bill says he can tighten the screw to even more boost if you're really intent on excitement.

The conversion to LPG uses a 19.3-gal tank located approximately where Morgan fits its ordinary fuel tank. However, Bill notes that regulations dictate a 20 per cent air volume, so the tank's effective capacity is more like 15.4 gal. Also, with LPG refueling capacity being temperature-dependent, a

visit to the filling pump (actually, it's a valve) may result in less than 15.4 gal filling an empty tank. This activity is accompanied by considerable ceremony, starting with unlatching the rear-deck-mounted inlet and bleed valves, screwing in the filler nozzle, opening it and the bleed, then waiting until a piquant mist of propane from the latter signals a fill. And it costs quite a bit less than a visit to the gasoline pump: By shopping around, we found propane at 77c/gal. Now there's nostalgia, admittedly of the short-term variety.

By the way, our experience indicates that all propane or butane suppliers aren't necessarily able to refuel a car: this, because of motor-fuel licensing requirements. And there was one lad probably fresh from viewing a Great War dirigible movie, who refused to refuel our Moggie because thunderstorms were forecast.

The propane travels from the tank to a firewall-mounted vaporizer that's heated by engine coolant. There's also a vacuum-operated fuel lock/filter that keeps everything shut down when the engine isn't running. A single-barrel Impco propane carburetor replaces the V-8's two SUs fitted at Malvern Link and the propane system carries an automatic enrichment device for cold starts. Bill fiddles with the Lucas Opus electronic ignition to optimize the engine's propane compatibility: seems that propane wants more initial ignition advance than gasoline, but not quite as much overall. He says a turbo V-8 put out 200bhp at the rear wheels during dyno development, so we'd estimate 225bhp (SAE net) as peak horsepower at 5000rpm with the Rajay wastegate set for 6-psi maximum boost. Some added guesswork gives the estimate of 240 lb-ft of torque at 3000, but neither of these figures suggests the beautiful driveability and responsiveness of this engine.

In fact, the total experience of driving the Morgan evokes memories that have improved with age. You clamber into the cockpit by folding your right knee under the scuttle, tucking that foot down to where the pedals lurk, sliding in and maneuvring your left leg to follow. Do all this in the correct order, and you find yourself facing a handsome wood-rimmed Nardi wheel. In fact, you do more than face it – you're up near this lovely example of Italian craftsmanship. But not to worry, because once you experience Morgan steering, you'll realize that laid-back straight-arm driving is for sissies. This is steering that exercises shoulder muscles not just biceps.

The ignition switch is hidden beneath the dash, and the first few times it takes a couple tries to get the key in it. Evidently a Morgan concession to anti-theft considerations, and apparently the only one because with no outside door handles the locking latches inside seem awfully silly. All this can get reasonably complicated with the top and side curtains in place: Whether the car is locked or not, you slide a plastic panel of the side curtain open, reach in, fumble around a bit and unlatch the door. Speaking of top and side curtains, we can note that the Moggie's are exemplary of what English weather protection used to be. And honestly, it's not all that difficult to assemble or disassemble, roughly midway between the superb ease of a Fiat Spider's, say, and the Erector-Set fiddling of a Jeep CJ's. Having the top up is a mixed blessing, however. It does give some space behind the seats for storage, but anyone except for the shortest driver gets only crooked-head side glances at whatever might be happening to the right or left. And the bowing-out, flapping and general lack of seal had our Engineering Editor calling his 90-mph sound level measurement of 98dBA 'the positive hinges of hell'. No matter, chaps: the best course is to leave the top and side curtains at home in the garage anyway.

Top up or down, the Morgan's cockpit is a nice snug one. Directly ahead of the driver is full instrumentation, including a speedometer calibrated to 170mph, a Smiths unit evidently left over from the D-Type Jaguar or some such. You like to think Peter Morgan got a deal on the last batch of them. The steering column stalks are straight out of JRT right-hand-drive models, with the directionals/high beam/flasher/horn on the right and wiper/washers on the left. The handbrake along the driveshaft tunnel is of the genuine fly-off variety: its button locks it on; a quick pull rearward and release unlock it. And also down on the tunnel is a device resembling a foot-actuated dimmer switch. This is Morgan's One-Shot Auto-Lube control, the depression of which causes a squirt of engine lube to pass onto the sliding-pillar front suspension. It's the only thing that's automatic about a Morgan's lubrication, what with a total of 10 sites around the car profiting from grease-up every 3000 miles.

But enough of these details. A twist of the key, and the V-8 throbs to life. Snick the stubby lever into 1st, ease out the clutch, and you're burbling away, looking down that long louvred bonnet at one of the classic views in motoring. Stomp the throttle (one of those little roller types many of us learned to heel-and-toe with), and gobs of torque at the bottom end turn into raspy turbo power as the revs build past 3000. Redundant though they may be with all this power, the gear ratios are nicely spaced and it's a gearbox you enjoy shifting for the sheer pleasure of it all. And if you get downright serious, you can go from 0 to 60mph in 6.8 seconds and turn the standing quarter mile in 15.1 sec at 93.5mph.

As for ride and handling, you've got to remember that terms like oversteer, understeer and suspension compliance were coined long after key elements of the Morgan were already in place. Essentially, it's a car that likes to wash out its front end first, although there's enough power available to provoke the rear end too. From a relatively rearward seating position, you sense the road at all

Price

List price, FOB San Francisco	$23,500	
Price as tested	$27,625	

Price as tested includes standard equipment (propane conversions, turbo sys ($2500), aluminium alloy body ($550), adj seats ($350), brown top, tonneau cover and side curtains ($350), Nardi steering wheel ($185), badge bar & badges ($115), decambered front suspension ($75)

Importer

Isis Imports, Ltd. Inc, PO Box 2290, US Custom House, San Francisco, Calif. 94126

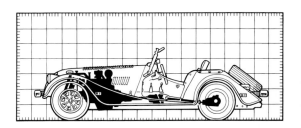

General

Curb weight, lb/kg	2285	1037
test weight	2475	1124
Weight dist (with driver), f/r %		44/56
Wheelbase in/mm	99.0	2515
Track, front/rear	52.0/53.0	1321/1346
Length	157.0	3988
Width	62.0	1575
Height	52.0	1321
Ground clearance	6.0	152
Overhang, f/r	23.5/34.5	597/876
Trunk space, cu ft/liters	4.4	125
Fuel capacity, US gal/litres	15.4	58

Instrumentation

Instruments: 170-mph speedo, 7000-rpm tach, 99,999 odo, 999.9 trip odo, oil press., coolant temp, turbo boost, voltmeter, fuel level.
Warning lights: oil press., brake sys, hazard, seatbelts, high beam, directionals.

Engine

Type	ohv V-8
Bore × stroke, in/mm	3.50 × 2.80, 88.9 × 71.1
Displacement, cu in/cc	215, 3528
Compression ratio	9.4:1
Bhp @ rpm, SAE net/kW	est 225/168 @ 5000
Equivalent mph/km/h	128/207
Torque @ rpm, lb ft/Nm	est 240/325 @ 3000
Equivalent mph/km/h	77/124
Carburetion	Impco propane (1V)
Fuel requirement	propane/butane, 105-oct
Exhaust emission control equipment	None

Drivetrain

Transmission		5-sp manual
Gear ratios: 5th (0.83)		2.76:1
4th (1.00)		3.31:1
3rd (1.40)		4.62:1
2nd (2.08)		6.90:1
1st (3.32)		10.99:1
Final drive ratio		3.31:1

Accommodation

Seating capacity, persons	2
Head room, in/mm	37.5, 953
Seat width	2 × 19.5, 2 × 495
Seat back adjustment, deg	40

Chassis & Body

Layout	front engine/rear drive
Body/frame	separate, aluminium & steel on ash/steel
Brake system	11.0in (279mm) discs front
	9.0in × 1.8in (229 × 46mm) drums rear
Swept area, sq in/sq cm	226/1458
Wheels	cast alloy, 14 × 6
Tires	Michelin XWX, 195VR-14
Steering type	cam & peg
Overall ratio	na
Turns, lock-to-lock	2.2
Turning circle, ft/m	38.0/11.6

Front suspension: vertical sliding pillars, coil springs, tube shocks
Rear suspension: live axle on leaf springs, lever-action shocks

Maintenance

Service intervals, mi:	
Oil filter change	5000/5000
Chassis lube	3000
Tuneup	20,000
Warranty, mo/mi	12/12,000

Calculated Data

Lb/bhp (test weight)	11.0
Mph/1000rpm (5th gear)	25.5
Engine revs/mi (60mph)	2350
Piston travel, ft/mi	1095
R&T steering index	0.84
Brake swept area, sq in/ton	183

four corners and watch that lovely bonnet bob up and down, back and forth. All the while, you come to appreciate the close-to-the-wheel seating because the Moggie's cam-and-peg steering is extremely stiff and notchy, just about impossible to turn at rest and affected

with that characteristic remembered by MG TC drivers of combining lots of center free-play with very abrupt response once the slack is used up.

At its lofty top speed, and this car will redline 4th fairly easily, things get busy indeed. Driven more sedately, though, the Morgan provides excellent input to the driver and it responds decently despite its heavy controls. It enjoyed a tight line through our slalom, for instance, with absolutely no lean and little squirts of power between pylons as it posted a commendably quick 61.1mph. It bobbed its bonnet around our skidpad with a

lateral acceleration of 0.791g. Not bad for Thirties suspension, eh? Yet both of these are smooth-surface evaluations in which the Morgan's ample tire patches, predictable understeer and quick steering fill the bill. No staff member felt it would be anything but a handful down a less than smooth twisty road at speed, and sure enough it was, exhibiting behavior that one staff member termed 'St Malvern's Dance.'

The brakes reinforce this feeling of vintage motoring. Even though they're modern enough disc/drum combinations, they're free of vacuum assist and required a super-high 60-lb pedal pressure for our 0.5g stops. However, they pull the car down evenly with excellent control, and distances from 60 and 80mph were quite short at 157 and 269ft respectively. On heavy braking, the front end chatters up and down as the sliding-pillar structure deflects in reaction to the most definitely post-vintage width of the Michelin XWX195VR-15s. Bill Fink notes that he's experimented with added bracing of the front end that mitigates this hopping routine.

But you can bet he's not going to change any of the essential features, because Bill is a believer. And after spending some time with this latest Morgan, we definitely understand its attraction. Modern machinery is easier to drive, but what's often traded away is the enjoyment of challenge and accomplishment. To drive a Morgan properly, you get to forget your daily concerns: you have to concentrate on the car and its operation. For a while there, with the louvred bonnet leading the way, the transmission tunnel warming your right leg and the cold wind tousling your hair, you and the Morgan are very good friends indeed.

Road Test Results

Acceleration

Time to distance, sec:	
0–100ft	3.3
0–500ft	8.3
0–1320ft (¼ mi)	15.1
Speed at end of ¼ mi, mph	93.5
Time to speed, sec:	
0–30mph	2.7
0–60mph	6.8
0–100	18.0

Speeds in Gears

5th gear (5000rpm)	128
4th (5500)	117
3rd (5500)	81
2nd (5500)	56
1st (5500)	35

Fuel Economy

Normal driving, mpg	16.0
Cruising range, mi (1 gal res)	230

Handling

Lateral accel, 100ft radius, g	0.791
Speed thru 700ft slalom, mph	61.1

Brakes

Minimum stopping distances, ft:	
From 60mph	157
From 80mph	269
Control in panic stop	very good
Pedal effort for 0.5g stop, lb	60
Fade: percent increase in pedal effort to maintain 0.5g deceleration in 6 stops from 60mph	8
Parking: hold 30% grade?	yes
Overall brake rating	very good

Interior Noise

Idle in neutral, dBA	65
Maximum, 1st gear	90
Constant 30mph	82
50mph	86
70mph	93
90mph	98

Speedometer Error

30mph indicated is actually	27.5
60mph	54.6
80mph	73.1

PLUS 8 BODY CHANGES

Just as the engine capacity of the V8 has crept up over the years, so too has the Plus 8 body grown wider by degrees, in order to accommodate wider track suspension layout and the expansion of tyre width. The three evolutions took place in 1973, 1977, and 1982. Although the cowl and scuttle panels have always been made of steel for rigidity, an aluminium body or wings or body only could be specified. The Plus 8 had two fuel fillers, removing the Morgan badging from the rear panel, and the three wiper blades are a current feature. Alloy bumpers replaced overriders at the rear in 1977, although chromed ones were always optional back and front. The wider body of the Plus 8 allowed greater freedom of movement for the occupants, although this was compromised slightly by the gearbox housing. Bucket seats by Restall were fitted at the recommendation of Maurice Owen, as they provided better support in high speed cornering. Creature comforts took a step forward with the fitting of a fresh air heater to replace the 'fug-stirrer' in 1973, and carpets were introduced the following year. Trimmed storage recesses were cut in the inner door panels. The dash was redesigned in 1977, pairing the speedo with the tacho which alone had previously occupied the driver's attention, the speedo being rather closer to the passenger's line of vision in earlier models. I recall the original Alfa

Romeo Alfetta GTV instrumentation was similarly designed; there's nothing like pandering to the driver's best sporting instincts!

The ancillary lighting and indicators have altered subtly over the years, swapping shapes and locations according to practicalities and regulations, not the least of which were the US Federal safety laws with which it was necessary to comply to re-establish a market in the States. Nothing sets a car off better than a good set of wheels, although the Morgan is distinctive enough not to have too many worries in this department. Plus 8 wheels have passed through four metamorphoses, from 15 × 5½in finned cast alloy between 1968 and 1976, shod with 185–VR15 Dunlop SP Sport tyres, and neater 14 × 6in Milrace alloys with 195– or 205–VR14 Dunlops from 1977 to 1982; then reverting in 1982 to alloys similar to the first type, now 15 × 6½ in, and post 1987 to 15 × 6in, cast with the Morgan Motor Company name and featuring a company badge and Plus 8 logo in the centre cap. Tyres have been 205/60–VR 15 low-profile jobs, firstly Pirelli P6s, then Avon from 1986 to 1988, and Uniroyals between 1988 and 1990, and reverting to Pirelli's P600 with the 3.9-litre car. From 1993 a stronger stainless-steel 72-spoke wire wheel has been available, developed for

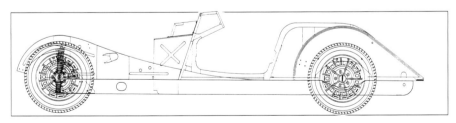

Outline drawing of the Plus 8 chassis and frame.

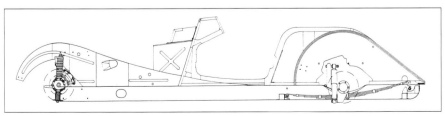

CAD side view of Plus 8 chassis and frame, showing front and rear suspension.

Hard tops

Consider the traditional image of the typical Morgan driver, and many would see a hairy-chested country type, biceps bulging and hair blowing in the slipstream. Look at the 1970s photo of John Macdonald and co lined up beside their cars in the competition section, and you will see it is not an inaccurate picture. Morgan lore has it that hoods should be worn down at all times. Less hardy souls who admire the performance and handling but have become softened through decadent hot-hatchery can always resort to a hard top, turning their Morgan into the thinking man's saloon car.

The factory is not geared up to produce fibreglass items, although aluminium could be used, just like the lid TOC 258 wore at Le Mans in 1962. It was for exactly this use that Rutherford Engineering, run by Dave Rutherford, began making hard tops in 1978; the factory needed a lid for MMC 11 to counteract the buffeting effect of high speed wind resistance, and Rutherford provided exactly what was wanted.

Hard tops can be bought by mail order, and indeed, Rutherford exports many to Germany. Ideally he needs the customer to leave his car for a morning so the top can be matched to the car; it's a bit like needing a new bonnet if your wings get damaged; the hard top will fit more snugly if it is pruned slightly to the individual car. Once that has been done, it can be removed or replaced in a matter of minutes. The top seals onto the windscreen, and is tensioned by stainless steel rods at each side, which are attached by wing-nuts under the dashboard. At the back, it is held in place by stainless steel over-centre clips and aluminium brackets located behind the doors. Dave Rutherford explained that many of his customers take out the hood during the winter when the top is in use because it provides more space behind the seats.

Hard tops are finished in gloss white, with a smooth white interior. Prices ranged in 1993 from £340 plus VAT for a 4/4 or Plus 4 top, and £330 for a Plus 8, to £450 for the very practical four-seater version. £95 buys an optional headlining, and the fitting charge is £75. For a little extra, hard tops can be modified to fit cars built before 1970, and of course there is a carriage charge if buying by mail order. Fibreglass wings are also available, and they are a more economical way of replacing extremities damaged in competition. Rutherford Engineering also specializes in supplying after-market suspension kits, including negative camber plates for road and track, uprated suspension components including Panhard rods and telescopic damper conversion kits for rear suspension mountings. Most Morgan agents will also assist in modifying cars for greater performance and improved handling, particularly those involved in competition themselves.

Morgan by Motor Wheel Services. At 16 × 7in, this can accommodate even wider rubber, and it was immediately welcomed in Germany where they love both wire spokes and wide wheels. At the time of writing, there were plans for a 25th Anniversary Plus 8, to be launched in August 1993, and fitted with centre-lock alloy wheels and a special paint finish. The Plus 8 has itself been getting progressively wider, although it is not as wide as some modern cars; but the extra width wheel undoubtedly helps the handling. There is now a huge difference between the behaviour of Plus 8 and 4/4, since the Plus 8 is six inches the wider car. Although the 4/4's handling is much more progressive, its ultimate cornering ability is about half that of the Plus 8.

CHANGES IN THE 4/4 SPECIFICATION

The 4/4 1600 was originally offered in two-

or four-seater form, either as standard or in competition trim, and since most customers wanted the latter, that became standard fare from 1971. Anti-burst door locks were mandatory from then, sourced from Land Rover, and bucket seats, in Connolly hide, could be had instead of the long-serving bench type. A customer could specify an aluminium body and wings from 1977, and Charles Morgan is of the opinion that there is no other option for a sports car, although it may dent slightly more easily than steel. The wider wings derived from the re-introduced Plus 4 were also available, and Charles and Works Manager Mark Aston also brought in long-overdue rot and corrosion measures in October 1986, which included dipping the frames in Cuprisol, and spraying the wings and doors separately from the rest of the car. The chassis could either be powder-coated or hot-dip galvanized if required; rather like a volcanic eruption, the latter is a spectacular process to observe. Morgan now got its own epoxy powder-coating plant so that all those unnoticed items like bulkheads, chassis hoops, engine mounting brackets and valances could be protected. This attention to problem-free bodywork was extended to the use of zinc-plated screws and fasteners. Modern ICI 2K two-pack was now the order of the day, replacing the old cellulose.

After a very long production run, the 1600 crossflow engine was phased out by 1984 when gearbox supply had dried up due to Ford going transverse with its Escort engine mountings. Morgan turned to Fiat for a supply of 131 Mirafiori 1,584cc twin-cams, similar to those which had powered the Fiat 124 Sport Spider. They were mated to five-speed Abarth gearboxes, units which were descended from the Fiat Abarth Spider Rallye World Rally Championship contenders from the early 1970s. The story has passed into legend that a senior Ford executive with a 4/4 on order was so incensed at discovering a Fiat power unit installed in the car on display at the Motor Show that he persuaded his directors at Ford to allow Morgan to re-engineer the new 1,597cc CVH engine to take the Cortina gearbox. In the event, Ford took a chassis away and did the conversion themselves using a Capri bell-housing and a Morgan-designed flywheel. It also required a revised bulkhead and different engine mountings. In the event, only 92 Fiat 1600 twin-cam engined cars were built, because cheaper Ford-engined cars were always available at the same time. There was never any external distinguishing badge to show which engine was fitted, although the exhaust from the Ford engine emerged on the nearside rear, and that of the Fiat the offside. From 1984, the 4/4 with CVH engine was equipped with the Sierra's five-speed gearbox, and in 1986, the Cam Gears steering box was replaced with the Gemmer recirculating ball type. The 4/4

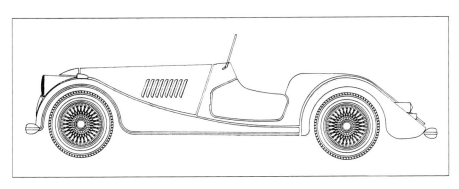

CAD-generated drawing of a 4/4 two-seater.

saga continued with Ford's lean-burn version of the CVH unit available from 1987, superseded by the XR3i engine with catalyst from 1991. 1993 saw the introduction of the 1,800cc Zeta engine, calling into question the reduced gap in performance between the new Ford engine and the M16 unit of the Plus 4.

PLUS 4 RENAISSANCE

The Plus 4 reappeared in 1985 with the venerable fuel-injected 2-litre Fiat twin-cam engine (again similar to the unit used in the 131 Mirafiori saloons) and provided an interim model between the Plus 8 and 4/4.

4/4 1600 (1969–1992)

Layout & Chassis
Two- and four-seater sports; Z-section side-members, five welded box-section cross-members; detachable frame-front; powder-coated from 1986

Engine

Type	Ford Kent 2737E & 2737GT; 2265E from 1971
	Fiat twin-cam from 1981
	Ford CVH from 1982
Block material	Cast iron
Head material	Cast iron 'crossflow'
Cylinders	4 in-line
Cooling	Water
Bore and stroke	Kent: 81 × 77.7mm
	Fiat: 84 × 71.50mm
	CVH: 79.96 × 79.52mm
Capacity	Kent: 1,599cc
	Fiat: 1,584cc
	CVH: 1,597cc
Valves	8 ohv
Compression ratio	Ford: 9.5:1
	Fiat: 9:1
Carburettors	Kent 2737E: Zenith; 2737GT: Weber
	Fiat: Weber or Solex
	CVH: Weber; 'lean-burn' Weber from 1987
	CVH EFI: Weber/Marelli fuel-injection from 1991
Max. power (DIN)	2737E: 70bhp @ 4,750rpm
	2737GT: 95.5bhp @ 5,500rpm
	Fiat: 98bhp @ 6,000rpm
	CVH: 96bhp @ 6,000rpm
	CVH EFI: 100bhp @ 6,000rpm
Max. torque	CVH: 97lb/ft @ 4,000rpm
	CVH EFI: 102lb/ft @ 2,800rpm
Fuel capacity	12.5 gallons (56l), two-seater; 10 gallons (45l), four-seater

Brakes

Type	Girling dual-circuit hydraulic from 1971
Size	11in discs front, 9 × 1.75in drums rear, fly-off handbrake

To add some slight confusion, a handful of Fiat-engined Plus 4s were fitted with carburettors and were badged 4/4s. There were difficulties in dealing with a foreign engine supplier; the contacts were with Iveco, Fiat's UK truck subsidiary, (which was subsequently taken over by Ford), and although there were no fallings out, there was a feeling that there was a lack of commitment in Turin and indifferent paperwork and pricing policy. The demise of the Fiat gearbox was the final straw, and by 1988, Morgan was able to go native once again for the Plus 4 with the new 16-valve twin-cam 2.0-litre

Transmission

Clutch	7½in diameter diaphragm spring
Gearbox	Ford 4-speed
	Fiat-Abarth 5-speed
	Ford 5-speed
Ratios	Ford: 5th 0.83, 4th 1.0, 3rd 1.37, 2nd 1.97, 1st 3.65:1; Reverse 3.66:1
	Fiat: 5th 0.87, 4th 1.0, 3rd, 1.36, 2nd 2.05, 1st 3.61:1; Reverse 3.24:1
Final Drive	Prop-shaft with needle roller bearing universal joints; Salisbury axle with hypoid gears, ratio, 4.1:1

Suspension and Steering

Front	Sliding stub axles on king pin, coil springs, and Girling telescopic dampers
Rear	Semi-elliptic leaf springs with Armstrong lever-arm dampers; Silentbloc bushes
Steering	Cam Gears cam-and-peg; turning circle: 33ft (10m); Gemmer recirculating ball from 1986, turning circle: 32ft (9.7m)
Wheels	15 × 5.6in Dunlop disc to 1980, 72-spoke 4½J wires, 15in Rostyle from 1980–1990
Tyres	165 × 15 Pirelli Cinturato, Michelin, Uniroyal; 195/60VR 15 Avon if wide Plus 4 body specified
Rim width	5.6in steel, 4½J, 5in, 6in, wires or 5½in Rostyle

Dimensions (in/mm)

Track	
Front	Kent & Fiat: 47/1,194
	CVH: 48/1,219
Rear	49/1,245
Wheelbase	96/2,438
Overall length	Kent & Fiat: 144/3,658
	CVH: 153/3,886 (includes rear bumpers from 1977)
Overall width	Kent & Fiat: 56/1,422
	CVH: 57/1,448
Overall height	Two-seater: 52/1,321; four-seater: 54/1,372
Unladen weight	Two-seater: 1,912lb/860kg; four-seater: 2,024lb/911kg

			Morgan Performance Figures		
Model	**Engine Capacity**	**Output (bhp)**	**Max Speed mph (km/h)**	**0–60mph (0–96km/h)**	**Average mpg (l/100km)**
4/4 SI	1,122cc	34	78 (125)	28.4 secs	35 (8.08)
4/4 SI	1,267cc	38.8	80 (128)	25.0 secs	35 (8.08)
4/4 SII	1,172cc	36	70 (112)	29.4 secs	36 (7.86)
4/4 SIII	997cc	39	85 (136)	14.9 secs	30 (9.4)
4/4 SIV	1,340cc	62	90 (144)	13.7 secs	28 (10.1)
4/4 SV	1,498cc	65	98 (157)	10.9 secs	31.5 (8.9)
4/4 1600	1,599cc	70	102 (163)	11.0 secs	32 (8.8)
4/4 1600	1,584cc	98	106 (170)	10.3 secs	24.8 (11.4)
4/4 1600	1,597cc	96	106 (170)	9.0 secs	25.3 (11.2)
4/4 1800	1,796cc	130	120 (192)	8.9 secs	32 (8.8)
Plus 4	2,088cc	68	85 (136)	14.1 secs	25.6 (11.05)
Plus 4	1,991cc	98	96 (154)	13.3 secs	30 (9.4)
Plus 4	2,138cc	104	102 (163)	10.9 secs	26 (10.9)
Plus 4	1,995cc	122	119 (190)	8.7 secs	25 (11.3)
Plus 4	1,994cc	138	109 (174)	7.7 secs	30 (9.4)
Plus 8	3,528cc	151	124 (198)	6.5 secs	20 (14.1)
Plus 8	3,528cc	143	123 (197)	6.7 secs	18 (15.7)
Plus 8	3,528cc	155	124 (198)	6.5 secs	20.5 (13.8)
Plus 8	3,528cc	190	122 (195)	5.6 secs	20 (14.1)
Plus 8 (US)	3,528cc (propane)	225 (turbo)	128 (205)	6.8 secs	16 (17.7)
Plus 8	3,946cc	190	130 (208)	5.2 secs	25 (11.3)

Rover M16 engine, mated to the V8's five-speed SD1 gearbox. The 138 M16 engine was developed by Rover's Sivert Hildemark, a Swede who works with engineering supremo Alex Stephenson, who was also responsible for the Metro K-series engines. The original objective was to produce a lean-burn engine, and its swirling combustion technology and fuel efficiency won it a Design Council award. The Lucas electronic engine management system allowed a relatively high compression ratio of 10:1 for more efficient combustion. But it couldn't make it across the board in terms of temperature variations, so it had to be catalysed to comply with EEC noise and emission regulations. Its promise has come to fruition in the current T16 unit, available in the Plus 4 from 1992. Hildemark continues to develop these engines, and the 200 turbocharged T16 is a great performer; to give an idea of just how quick, in the Rover 220 Turbo Coupé its 0–60mph (0–96 km/h) time is 6.5 secs, and top speed is 147.6mph (237.5km/h).

At first it was possible to specify either the 4/4 chassis and body size or the larger Plus 8 for your Plus 4, but by the end of 1991 all Plus 4s were built on the Plus 8 chassis but with the narrower frame front. The Plus 4 therefore has a wider track than the 4/4, but it continues to use the 4/4 suspension layout. To improve weight distribution, the battery was moved under the rear seats in the four-seater car in 1989. All four-seaters are taller than two-seaters, by some two inches, and the windscreen is also taller. The rear seats

Morgan Production and Chassis Numbers

Model	Engine	First Number	Last Number	Total	Dates
4/4					
Series I	Coventry Climax & Standard Special	1	2081	1,315	Mar 1936–Feb 1951
Series II	Ford 100E	A200	A586	386	Oct 1955–Oct 1960
Series III	Anglia 105E	A590	A648	58	Oct 1960–Nov 1961
Series IV	Classic 109E	B650	B855	114	Oct 1961–Mar 1963
Series V	Cortina 116E	B856	B1495	639	Feb 1963–Mar 1968
1600	Ford Kent 2737E/2737GT 2265E from 1971	B1600	B5133	3,513	Feb 1968–Mar 1982
1600	Fiat	F6002	F6956	96	Nov 1981–Nov 1985
1600	Ford CVH	C6004	C8467	1,652	Mar 1982–Nov 1991
1600	Ford EFI	C8452	C8639	187	Nov 1991–Jan 1993
1800	Ford Zeta	Z			April 1993–
Plus 4					
	Vanguard	P2100	P3922**	799	Dec 1950–May 1958
	TR2	2750	3488	344	May 1954–Jun 1956
	TR3	3421	5574	1,808	Feb 1956–Feb 1964
	TR4	5136	6853	1,582	Jun 1962–Sep 1969
	Fiat	F6796	F7240	125*	Apr 1985–Jan 1987
	Rover M16	M7569	M8666	356	Jul 1988–Aug 1992
	Rover T16	T8681			August 1992–
Plus 8					
Moss Gearbox		R7000	R7494	494	Oct 1968–Sep 1972
4-speed Rover		7475	8186	711	Mar 1972–Jan 1977
5-speed		8200	9775	} 2,165	Jan 1977–Jan 1987
	3.5 inj.	9372	10,365	}	May 1984–Jun 1990
	3.9 inj.	10240			August 1989–

*Includes twelve 2.0-litre Fiat carburettor engines
**Last car with Vanguard engine, although general production stopped with chassis number 2756 in June 1954

are perched above the axle, and one benefit is that it enables children to sit up high and get a better view than they would in a regular saloon car. The Plus 4 four-seater is quite a big car, prompting the thought that it must be better value as you get more car for your money! However, the four-seater version of the Plus 4 was given a lower body profile in 1990.

THE CAR REGISTER

One of the endearing things about Morgan is that from the outset, every car they make has its particulars written down in copperplate longhand in a tome called the Car Register. Owners of older cars frequently write in asking for details, and there is a move to create a proper archive which could be consulted on a fee-paying basis. And who knows, a small museum might follow, featuring an audio-visuai display and three-wheelers one month and flat-rads the next! The Car Register reveals the chassis number, and until recently the gearbox number; it quotes paint colour and trim details, plus any faults corrected before delivery, and finally, the delivery address. Post-war chassis numbers were allocated when the car was about to be delivered, which was an improvement on the earlier system of ascribing the chassis number to the order, which produced a gap in the numbering system if an order was cancelled. Even so, strange anomalies occur, such as an unsold early fifties flat-radiator car failing to find an owner and thus leave the factory until long after the semi-cowled-radiator cars were in production; or conversely, a rolling chassis which actually left the factory destined for Italy and a fancy coachbuilt body, but returned to Malvern two years later, covered in dockside rust, for a rebuild and a proper, but later, Morgan body. It often happens that the numbering sequence is thrown simply because a car is waiting for an unusual or out-of-stock part, and it sits around in the factory as others are finished. When it emerges, certain components may be older than one might expect from the chassis number. But whatever becomes of it, every car built is part of Morgan's rich and continuously developing history.

2 An Overview

When I began my research for this book, Charles Morgan had just returned from a trip to Japan, and despite being a little jet-lagged, was full of his impressions of the Japanese Morgan club and the car market. In Japan there is a dedicated band of Morgan *aficionados* who would love to revert to aero screens and carburettors, competition roundels on the doors, to be accompanied by leather flying helmets and goggles no doubt, but legislation the world over means such cars cannot be built at the factory any more. So Morgan make three standardized models up to painting stage, and from thereon, the customer can specify how the finished car will look. There are aluminium or steel body options of course, 35,000 choices of colour, four types of seat, leather or PVC upholstery, wood or leather-covered dashboard, inside lights, hi-fi, and two types of hood material. It would naturally be easier for Morgan to standardize everything, even down to building just Plus 4s in Connaught green, but one of the joys of Morgans is the diversity and flexibility of choice.

Reflections on Japan served as a good introduction to an overview of how Morgan is doing today, since foreign sales are crucial. Not surprisingly, Japan is a prime target having one of the most buoyant economies in the world. The Japanese market takes twenty to twenty-five cars a year. Fifty-five per cent of all Morgan's production is exported, which was perfectly obvious as I toured the factory; I was struck by the number of left-hand drive cars in build.

TYPE APPROVAL

One of the problems of meeting the different safety regulations of individual foreign markets is obtaining 'type approval'. Scouting through the growing mountains of legislative paperwork and coming up with the best solutions give Charles Morgan and Works Manager Mark Aston plenty of headaches. The cost of development and testing has to be spread over a very small number of cars, but as far as the foreign bureaucrats are concerned, a Morgan is no different from a Ford or a Mercedes Benz; the same rules have to be followed. But whereas a £10,000 testing fee is amortized over millions of Escorts, it is two-thirds the price of one 4/4.

Interestingly enough, although a Morgan may look to some like a thirties car, it has to embody all the safety technology expected in a car of the nineties. The Morgan has therefore become more complex and difficult to build, which makes it remarkable that the workforce, numbering 130, has not increased accordingly. Stylistic evolution of cars in general has made life difficult for Morgan; as car rear ends have got higher and higher, so has the height of the rear lights, and the authorities wonder why not everyone has followed suit. Morgan has had to argue that this is not appropriate for its products, although the next round of legislation will necessitate a central rear light mounted above the spare wheel. There are other unseen standards to comply with. For example, exhaust emissions are measured between two bollards, and since a Morgan Plus 8 covers this distance faster than the Range Rover, it has to be quieter than the

Visitors' introduction to the factory is the cream-panelled reception room, decorated with paintings and boards commemorating the marque's sporting successes.

donor vehicle, and produce fewer emissions during the air-pollution test. The result is a cleaner car. Each foreign market has different criteria for granting import licences, and in Japan one car in ten is inspected; in Germany it was every one until recently. France is more lenient, checking just the first of every model. There is now a GB Type Approval number for low-volume manufacturers, which is not recognized abroad, because tests are more lenient than the full EEC standards. This is not a lot of good to Morgan, which depends heavily on foreign sales. But having complied with EEC Regulations, there are separate homologation tests to be done to get the cars into Sweden, Switzerland, the USA and Japan. This could be construed as a kind of protectionism, whereby foreign imports are excluded by legislation. Morgan is fortunate in having agents who are themselves foreign nationals, which assists the importation procedures; transport authorities are linked with police and customs. There is a tidy

consistency about Morgan production so that foreign authorities are never suddenly confronted with fifty extra cars to import. Aspects of legislation where homologation tests differ are in emissions, durability and longevity of catalytic equipment, and noise. There is a positive aspect to this, as the overall effect is to maintain Morgan's engineering quality at world-class standards.

It is vital that each car in build is correctly identified as to which country it is destined for, because of the type approval anomalies from market to market. The 4/4 cannot be sold in Japan because the centre-lock wheelnuts protrude outside the wheelarches, so a Japanese customer will have to take the wide-bodied Plus 4 with the current Ford engine in order to accommodate the 4/4 wheelnuts. A fair amount of Morgan's emissions testing is done in Germany, where the TUV are very efficient and have the testing down to a fine art, if not the paperwork, which is naturally in German and thus a headache for Morgan.

4/4 (1993 onwards)

Layout & Chassis
Front-engine rear-drive two- and four-seater sports; deep Z-section with five boxed or tubular cross-members and easily detachable frame-front

Engine
Type	Ford Zeta in-line twin-cam
Block material	Cast iron with cast aluminium sump
Head material	Aluminium alloy
Cylinders	4 in-line
Cooling	Water
Bore and stroke	88.0×80.6mm
Capacity	1,796cc
Valves	16 Dohc with hydraulic tappets
Compression ratio	10.0:1
Carburettor	Sequential fuel-injection with full electronic management, Ford EEC-IV computer
Max. power (DIN)	130bhp @ 6,250rpm
Max. torque	120lb/ft @ 4,500rpm
Fuel capacity	12.5 gallons (56l)

Transmission
Gearbox	Ford/Powrtorque 5-speed and reverse
Ratios	5th 0.85:1, 4th 1.05:1, 3rd 1.48:1, 2nd 2.14:1, 1st 3.23:1
Final Drive	3.82:1

Suspension and Steering
Front	Independent by vertical coil springs on sliding axle pin, telescopic gas-filled dampers
Rear	Semi-elliptic rear springs with Armstrong lever-arm hydraulic dampers
Steering	Gemmer recirculating ball; turning circle 32ft (9.7m)
Tyres	165SR $\times$ 15 or 195/60VR $\times$ 15
Wheels	Centre-lock wire wheels on Rudge hubs
Rim width	5in or 6in

Brakes
Type	Girling hydraulic dual-circuit
Size	11in diameter discs front, 9×1.75in drums at rear, fly-off handbrake

Dimensions (in/mm)
Track	
Front	48/1,219
Rear	49/1,245
Wheelbase	96/2,438
Overall length	153/3,886
Overall width	57/1,448
Overall height	52/1,321
Unladen weight	1,910lb/868kg

The company's German agents help here, and Charles Morgan is quick to sing the praises of his agents worldwide. (Note the use of 'agents' rather than 'dealers'.) They were very much instrumental in getting sales moving again after the slump of the mid-1960s, and have tended to be Morgan fanatics first and Morgan agents second, which has meant they have enhanced the marque's reputation considerably. Agencies are without exception well run and administered, with service levels very high. For example, a Dane with a second-hand Plus 8 in Tokyo reported a distributor problem and within an hour, not one but two mechanics arrived at his flat; one to speak English and one to mend the car. This is typical of the Morgan's *esprit de corps*.

SAFETY MEASURES

Proper thick-section aluminium door beams will follow the airbags through the homologation process. Prior to 1993, any side intrusion was picked up by the rear wheelarch and the chassis, which afforded some protection to the occupants; the door beam will extend the cover. This places Morgan five years ahead of the game, as only a handful of the European makers, including Ford, GM and Volvo, have any form of door beam. Amongst the small developments under way, perhaps the most important is the fitting of an airbag in the steering wheel boss for the US market. This entails a comprehensive test programme, and involves crashing a mock-up Morgan body into a barrier about twenty times. A dummy records the effects of the airbag in limiting injury. This is done at MIRA under very stringent monitoring. There were initial reservations about putting it in a Morgan because of the number of cars that are involved in competition; to have an airbag go off during a 'moment' at Woodcote or

Paddock Bend would prove mighty embarrassing. But apparently they only stay inflated for 0.1 seconds, so it would hardly be noticed as visibility is not impaired. The bag pressure is related to the impact ratio of each particular car. The only implication for Morgan is that the seat has had to be angled slightly to prevent any possibility of the driver submarining under the airbag. 'Basically, once you've got your Morgan you can do what you like with it,' says Charles. So anyone set against airbags could simply swap the standard product for a Nardi wheel.

In Germany, all such extras are monitored in an MOT test which happens not after three years but when the car is first registered. So tyres and other running gear are checked. In the UK there is a flourishing trade in 'aftermarket' extras for Morgans, such as fold-flat screens, hard tops, stainless steel bonnet stays, light housings, uprated engines, and some people go in for suspension modifications. Taken to its ultimate, it is possible to double the price of a Plus 8 by equipping it with a supercharged 4.5-litre engine and other fine-tuned performance modifications, although this will probably be a competition car, on which everything can be altered so the running gear suits individual circuits.

PRODUCTION CYCLE

It takes about ten weeks for a car to progress through the production cycle. After passing out from the chassis assembly shop, the cars are likely to become separated from the batch they started with due to changes in specification and component variations and supply. But each car will pass through ten different departments during its gestation from bare chassis to pristine runner, and there are three back-up departments which provide input. After a while, even blindfold

Morgans have always cultivated a competition heritage, perpetuated by this trialling 1936 4-4 two-seater. Lessons learned in competition are applied to the production cars.

you could recognize your whereabouts in the factory, because each workshop has its own distinctive aroma. There's solvent in the paint shop, scorched wood and sawdust in the wood shop, Swarfega in the machine shop, leather in trim, and so on. Ten cars are completed every week, and since most operations take a week and paint a bit longer, there are roughly 100 vehicles in build at any given time.

Weekly production should work out at three each week of the Plus 4 and 4/4, and four of the Plus 8, but being a small company, Morgan is rather in the hands of its suppliers, who may not always see Morgan as their most important customer. Morgan is extremely fortunate in having its own machine shop which provides the bulk of the cars' smaller components. Surprisingly, it is most often engines and back axles which fail to come through on schedule, so it is the large suppliers rather than the small ones who foul up. As a result, there may be a shortage of certain components which forces them to halt production of whichever model they were destined for. As I researched this book, there was a slight hiccup over GKN-

sourced rear axles for a handful of Plus 4s, so for a short while they made just 4/4s and Plus 8s. The next hiatus was while they waited for the first consignment of Zeta engines for the 4/4; there was a slight question mark over the stated bhp figures which Morgan asked to be sorted out first. Overcoming such frustrations is part of Charles's job, and he sometimes feels they could be better sorted out by adopting the Japanese mass-production solution of stopping completely until the shortage or whatever is sorted out. Morgan is in the position of being able to make a Plus 4 if there is a problem with 4/4 component supply, so they need not actually stop completely. But things tend to average out, so that production is divided into thirds between the three basic models. Component supply is usually fine until a change of model or specification occurs. For example, the phasing out of the CVH-engined 4/4 involved buying in just a handful of items which would not be carried over into the new model. Stocks had not accurately matched the numbers of cars produced because Ford had not been able to supply them. Another shortage was the

---

Plus 4 (1985–1993)

Layout & Chassis
Sports two- or four-seater, deep Z-section with five boxed or tubular cross-members; as for Plus 8 from 1991

Engine

Type	1985: Fiat twin-cam
	1988: Rover M16 twin-cam
	1992: Rover T16 twin-cam
Block material	Cast iron
Head material	Aluminium alloy
Cylinders	4 in-line
Cooling	Water
Bore and stroke	84.5 × 89mm
Capacity	Fiat: 1,995
	Rover: 1,994cc
Valves	Dohc, 4 valves per cylinder
Compression ratio	Fiat: 9:1
	Rover: 10:1
Carburettors	Fiat: Bosch LE-Jetronic fuel-injection
	Rover: programmed ignition and Lucas L multi-point fuel-injection
Max. power (DIN)	Fiat: 122bhp @ 5,300rpm
	Rover: 138bhp @ 6,000rpm
Max. torque	Fiat: 129lb/ft @ 3,500rpm
	Rover: 131lb/ft @ 4,500rpm
Fuel capacity	Two-seater: 12.5 gallons (56l), four-seater: 10 gallons (45l)

Brakes

Type	Girling hydraulic dual-circuit
Size	11in discs front, 9 × 1.75in drums rear

---

petrol-tank filler necks, which contain a flap valve for the catalysed engines, sourced from the Montego. But Rover stopped making them, and for the 4/4s on the end of the line, they had to be sourced elsewhere in a very small batch, and modified to fit the Morgan by the machine shop. Delivery of £40,000 worth of cars was held up by a couple of filler tubes worth £3.50 each. Sometimes they may be stuck for little things for just one car, like a speedo cable or sidescreen brackets, and have to manufacture these in the machine shop.

The various workshops are also manufacturing stock for the spares department, which under Paul Trussler is being built up so that a reasonable stock is kept on the shelves for owners and agents, and as a hedge against unexpected shortages in production. 'There is no point in building cars unless you can supply spare parts,' is his view. Spares were previously only made to order, but again, as specifications change there has to be a balance; there is no point in keeping masses of idle stock.

Profit margins on each model are such

Transmission

Clutch	Fiat & Rover: hydraulic 7½in single dry plate
Gearbox	Fiat: 5-speed ex-125 special
	Rover: 5-speed ex-Plus 8
Ratios	Fiat: 5th 0.83, 4th 1.0, 3rd 1.36, 2nd 2.05, 1st 3.6:1; Reverse 3.24:1
	Rover: 5th 0.792, 4th 1.0, 3rd 1.396, 2nd 2.087, 1st 3.32:1;
	Reverse 3.42:1
Final Drive	Salisbury rear axle with hypoid gears, ratios: Fiat 4.1:1, Rover: 3.73:1

Suspension and Steering

Front	Independent by vertical coil springs on sliding stub axle; telescopic gas-filled dampers
Rear	Semi-elliptical rear springs; Armstrong lever-arm dampers; gas-filled telescopic dampers from 1992
Steering	Gemmer recirculating ball
	Jack Knight rack-and-pinion optional from 1991
Tyres	195/60VR × 15 Avon Turbospeed radials, tubed
Wheels	'Cobra style' centre-lock wire spoke on Rudge hubs
Rim width	6in

Dimensions (in/mm)

Track	
Front	50.5/1,283
Rear	51.5/1,308
Wheelbase	96/2,438
Overall length	153/3,886
Overall width	57/1,448
Overall height	50/1,270 two-seater, 52/1,321 four-seater
Unladen weight	2,002lb/910kg two-seater, 2,156lb/980kg four-seater

that the company would make most money if it built nothing but Plus 8s, but they acknowledge that this would be unwise in the long term. The official estimate is that about twenty per cent of 4/4 and Plus 4 production is made up of four-seater cars, although there seemed to me to be rather more than that when I was doing my research around the factory. Now the Plus 4 is built on the Plus 8 chassis, the four-seater version has increased legroom and seating in the back; a longer door and low-set rear seat are waiting in the wings, so that the four-seater of the future will be just that and not a two-plus-two where the rear passengers are perched precariously above the axle; this was why there was never officially a Plus 8 with four seats: so much torque could have the passengers flat on their backs in the road as the car disappeared in a cloud of dust.

DEVELOPMENTS AT MORGAN

Coachbuilding the car in wood brings into

Among the valuable skills at the Morgan factory is the ability to re-panel a car by eye; in this case it is works racer MMC 11.

play all sorts of different factors and issues which other cars do not have; like seatbelt stresses and conservation problems. Customers' reactions and criticisms of the cars are taken seriously at Morgan, probably more so than any other motor manufacturer. Charles makes a point of ringing a random selection of new owners after nine months to find out if they have had any problems, and at club meetings he is constantly buttonholed by owners with comments and ideas to put forward. The racing side is seen as an important way of trying new products like shock absorbers and putting components through far more arduous treatment than hours of testing at MIRA. Information discovered during racing is ploughed back into the road cars. There are many examples of racing improving the breed, and with materials improving this is still happening. There is an exotic works development car too; Charles has a blue Plus 8 which is virtually a pastiche of a factory car; it sits

low and its chassis is aluminium honeycomb sandwich, and the bonnet has no louvres. Although the shape is the same, it illustrates the fact that nothing stands still at Morgan. They may not produce a brand-new model very often, but there is a constant stream of improvements to the design. People don't see the shape changing, so they assume nothing much is going on, but to drive even a ten-year-old Plus 8 against a new one is like comparing chalk and cheese. There are visual differences too. Putting the wire wheels on the Plus 8 alters the appearance quite dramatically. And the dimensions of the Plus 8 and 4/4 are quite different anyway.

One of these changes is to the rear suspension. The Plus 4 and Plus 8's rear gas-filled shock absorbers are made by Gabriel in the USA, and are a huge improvement on the old lever arm dampers, and also the hydraulic units. Improvements in steel wire for coil springs has given the latest cars coil springs which last longer and give a more pliant ride. Some aspects are cosmetic. One tends to take things like bumpers for granted, but Charles believes the front bumper lets the car down badly, although it is an expensive and relatively complex piece of aluminium. It is light, yet strong, but because it is only anodized rather than chromed, it does not fit with the rest of the car. Two designs are under appraisal at present from two different suppliers. Charles has a scheme in mind to mould the bumper to follow the wing and grille contours across the front of the car. There may be a glint of chrome about it too. He makes it clear he considers such alterations very carefully and is keen to distance himself from the methods of TVR's Peter Wheeler, who is on record as saying that his dog designed the frontal aspect of the Griffith by biting a chunk out of the mock-up. 'It must be very nice running a factory like that,' he joked, 'but I wouldn't personally think that was the way to do it!'

Aside from such amiable rivalry, there is no chance of Morgans ever getting the kind of monstrosity which despoiled the MGB or Fiat 124 Spider in the name of Federal regulations and US sales. Having said that, Californian importer Bill Fink was having to incorporate VW Golf (Rabbit in the States) impact buffers and lift the bumper height of his butane LPG-fuelled Plus 8s by a few inches, as far back as 1980, but he got away with the aesthetics, and a turbo gave him the appropriate performance. Californian legislation forces him to fit a central stalk-mounted rear light sourced from a Porsche 928.

From a practical point of view, the car is constantly being asked to do more and more stressful things, with increases in torque and performance happening all the time. Now the 4/4 has the 1,800 Zeta engine, which is seen as the optimum engine choice for Morgan's basic car. It was felt that the old CVH-engined 4/4 was getting outclassed by some of the GTi brigade, although one would hardly buy a Morgan to sink into that particular trough. But there were other small sports cars like the MX–5, Caterham Seven, TVR–S and the Reliant Scimitar turbo which could put it in the shade performance-wise, although of course the Plus 4 would settle with these. The continuing role of the 4/4 is of a traditional Morgan, what the older employees in the factory refer to as the 'two-seater', with the narrower body, taller tyres, and tail-out handling characteristics. With an 1,800cc engine, this becomes very much more of a fun activity. And at last, Ford has produced a smooth-running engine with excellent fuel economy and emissions standards. The 4/4 has always been a popular car in countries where servicing and parts supply was marginal, but at least Ford components were available and reasonably cheap, and local garages could cope with Ford running gear. It thus remains an important car for Morgan, being popular in Japan for reasons of its traditional appearance as much as ease of maintenance.

But isn't the 1,800cc twin-cam engine too close to the 16-valve 2-litre T16 unit in terms of performance and the capacity gap between engine sizes of only 200cc? Charles Morgan's response is that the two engines may be fairly close now, but forthcoming developments by Rover will take the T16's capabilities into a different league. My feeling is that Charles sees the Plus 4 as the family Morgan, and is keen to develop its potential as a four-seater. We have already seen how the four-seater has undergone relatively major changes to increase practicality. The Plus 8 chassis has given greater width and allowed the seats to be lowered, and proper seatbelts can be fitted in the back. Probably drawing on his own experience with a young family, Charles considers it important to develop the model as there is a strong market for such a car. It is lighter

Racing is a way of learning more about what the cars will do, and of testing components more vigorously than hours at MIRA: this is the Libra Motive Plus 8 campaigned in 1991 and 1992 by Malcolm Paul in the 750 Motor Club's Roadsports series; it was fitted with a 4.2-litre engine for 1993.

than the Plus 8, but quick enough and plenty strong enough to carry four people. He has doubts about running such a fast car on the current tyres, and it may be necessary to go to the Plus 8's 205/60×15s. Charles would prefer to rationalize production to just the one four-seater model based on the Plus 4 with its extra space in the back and lap-and-diagonal seatbelts for rear seat passengers. So from 1993, you will not be able to order a four-seater 4/4.

In the machine shop, components start with sturdy drop-forgings which have been in use for a very long time. They are known quantities, and Tony Newman and his team know exactly how they are going to machine up and behave in certain situations. Strength in these items is vital, and although of course new items can be designed, it is very difficult to evaluate them in all the different circumstances they will encounter during the life of the car. 'The company uses a lot of drop-forgings,' says Charles. 'Although they're relatively heavy, if the design is right, you can't get a stronger

piece of material.' These forgings come from Palmer's foundry in Worcester, and Morgan's exacting standards make them just about Palmer's most difficult customers. They also follow the practice of leaving them out in all weathers to harden the material.

WASTAGE

As Production Manager, Charles is concerned to eliminate wastage, spillage and stoppages in the factory. Having traced the optimum time it takes to build a car, based on the time actually spent working on a car and assuming no delays, Charles is tempted to go flat out on a fortnight's overtime, clear the backlog, and start from scratch aiming to keep to a certain schedule and see how long it lasts. He sees it as more important for people to work more slowly if anything to get a job right first time, rather than trying to go faster and risk making mistakes. As a way of rationalizing the assembly programme, he is looking at the possibility of

Plus 8 (1991–1993)

Layout & Chassis
Deep Z-shape section with five boxed or tubular cross-members; front-engine, rear-drive, two-seater sports

Engine
Type	Rover V8 petrol
Block material	Aluminium
Head material	Aluminium
Cylinders	8
Cooling	Water
Bore and stroke	94 × 71.12mm
Capacity	3,946cc
Main bearings	5
Valves	16 ohv, pushrod with hydraulic tappets
Compression ratio	9.35:1
Carburettor	Lucas 'Hotwire' Electronic Injection system
Max. power (DIN)	190bhp @ 4,750rpm
Max. torque	235lb/ft @ 2,600rpm
Fuel capacity	12 gallons (54l)

Transmission
Clutch	Single plate diaphragm spring
Gearbox	Rover 5-speed all synchromesh plus reverse
Ratios	5th 0.79:1, 4th 1.0:1, 3rd 1.39:1, 2nd 2.08:1, 1st 3.32:1; Reverse 3.42:1
Rear axle	Salisbury limited-slip differential, hypoid gears 3.31:1

Suspension and Steering
Front	Independent by vertical coil springs: telescopic gas dampers
Rear	Semi-elliptical rear springs with telescopic gas-filled dampers by Gabriel
Steering	Jack Knight rack-and-pinion; turning circle 38ft (11.6m)
Tyres	205/60VR × 15 Pirelli P600 radials
Wheels	15in cast alloy 5-stud or 16in centre-lock 72-spoke wire
Rim width	6.5in alloy or 7in wire spoke

Brakes
Type	Girling hydraulic dual-circuit
Size	11in discs front, 9 × 1.75in drums rear; fly-off handbrake

Dimensions (in/mm)
Track	
Front	53/1,346
Rear	54/1,372
Wheelbase	98/2,489
Overall length	156/3,962
Overall width	63/1,600
Overall height	48/1,219
Unladen weight	2,068lb/940kg

changing the procedure of the chassis assembly shop. Rather than gradually making up ten chassis over a five-day period, he thinks it may be better to concentrate on fettling one chassis at a time, so that a rolling chassis goes off to the wood shop the moment it is ready, instead of ten being sent off more or less all at once. Foreman David Day is dubious as to whether or not this will be any quicker, but it may be tried.

Another possibility to be considered might be the leather in the trim shop, which theoretically could be cut out for the seats and the interior before the car actually gets there. When we went to the trim shop to photograph the upholstering, there was nothing to shoot, although six bare cars sat waiting to be trimmed. The material was only just being cut out. Charles thinks that if the planning was better, implying computerized, perhaps Charlie Styles could get his team cutting before the cars leave the paint shop. He will have ordered the appropriate hides well in advance of course, but leather is very expensive, and an error in selection at the cutting stage would be unacceptably costly.

Some items of high value are supplied 'just in time'. Amongst these are Connolly hides, which is helpful to Morgan as the last thing they need is 10,000 hides in stock. There is more to it than Connolly's efficiency. It is to do with a relationship of trust built up between customer and supplier over a long period, where bills are paid promptly and goods delivered on time. There are spin-offs, in that the supplier might well see Morgan as a useful selling point for their product, and Rover gains some useful information from Morgan as a specialized test-bed for its engines. Suppliers are also welcome to use the car for promotional purposes. The aim is to develop a lasting relationship with suppliers so there is mutual understanding of each other's requirements.

Morgan is not averse to helping other small car manufacturers, seeing the existence of as many small makers as possible in the market-place as beneficial. Old sayings such as 'safety in numbers' and 'variety is the spice of life' come to mind, and there is nothing wrong with the spirit of that. To Morgan, the concept of the giant corporation swallowing up the small producers is a complete disaster. Although there may be short-term cost benefits in having one management team overseeing a number of different companies, there is frequently a loss of identity and direction. As soon as the giant comes along, expecting his way to be best, the small company's identity is as good as lost. Lotus for one has been completely castrated, and all that is left is the fading Chapman heritage, a racing bike and a Formula 1 team with the same name. Each small company contains its own core values, and has developed its own wealth of expertise and experience. The feeling at Morgan is, understandably, one of fierce defiance, based on the certainty that you are more flexible as a small company. As we saw in the historical chapter, there have only been two serious moves to acquire Morgan; once by Standard Triumph in the early 1950s and then by Rover in the early 1970s. Despite their undeniably valuable skills, happily, Morgan is probably too much of a commercial anachronism now to be coveted by a conglomerate.

Charles is unconvinced by arguments promoting economies of scale by merging with a larger manufacturer, because research, innovations and new product are much easier to achieve in smaller and more flexible organizations. There is physically less stock to move around in a company manufacturing 500 cars a year than one making 500 a day. The main problem a small manufacturer faces with changing a car's mechanical specification is getting type approval.

Charles's time is divided between over-

Because of their lightness, three-wheelers can brake later and go much deeper into a corner than the four-wheel opposition; this pair of Super Sports from 1930 and 1932 demonstrate their superiority during a VSCC race at Oulton Park in 1970.

seeing manufacture of the cars and the marketing side of things, which is also partly Derek Day's province; there is liaison with writers and journalists, customers and Morgan Clubs, advertising and sponsorship, and attendance at motor shows. He is currently concerned with protecting the company name and logo, which involves registering them worldwide, at vast expense in a number of categories. This guards against unsolicited use of the Morgan name, which sometimes happens in the promotion of unrelated and often trashy products. Some are of a very high quality, like some German spectacles I was shown with Morgan logo embossed in the frames, or the pedal cars of the Morgan Model Company. The other side of the coin is a French clothing company, keen to colonize the name 'Morgon', which Charles was less than happy about. '*Morgon de toi*' translates roughly as 'I'm mad about you.' Fickle fashion being transitory, I suggested that no one would have heard of them in ten years' time.

COMPUTERIZATION

Morgan's biggest project at the time of writing was the installation of a computerized stock control system. This involved training the operators, and is designed to ease access to information throughout all departments in the factory, as it is an integrated system. It will also facilitate forward planning of manufacture. Ultimately it will help in tracking cars as they go round the plant, which implies having a computer terminal in each workshop so that data can be fed in with the passage of each car. This is done now of course, visually and physically, and the introduction of a computer network will simply serve as a back-up. An integrated central database giving an overview of the bills of material of all current items in build and each car will make the company more efficient. At the moment, each department is thoroughly conversant with its own activities, but does not necessarily have a view of the scheme of things as a whole.

CAD, the high-tech drawing board of computer-aided design has been in use for a couple of years, run by toolmaker David Goodwin, and produces drawings for prototype parts and tools to be made in the machine shop. The company has bought a new range of Viglen computers using British-made Swan software package, which is integrated with Soye Sovereign accounting software.

With his sporting activities, Charles puts his own cars through their paces to provide food for thought about changes which could be made to them. He tries out various modifications suggested by the development shop, such as different shock absorbers or suspension arrangements, to see whether they work in everyday circumstances. Testing prototypes on the road, under licence, has always been a regular thing. Morgan is a member of MIRA (Motor Industry Research Association) and has access to the banked test track and proving grounds. Charles is still mindful of his grandfather's influence, of which one of the key lessons is a low power-to-weight ratio. There is no point having a sports car which weighs as much as the equivalent saloon. The ideal formula is a powerful engine, set low down in a torsionally rigid car, coupled with light weight. The sports car has severe problems with torsional rigidity because it has no roof, and that is why they are relatively heavy compared with saloons. The BMW Z1 was meant to be state-of-the-art in the mid-1980s, yet it was heavier than the regular 3-Series BMW saloon. By using new materials, the sports car builder can get weight down.

LESSONS FROM THE PAST

In many ways these desirable qualities were exemplified by the three-wheelers of the 1920s, where the weight balance was over the front wheels and torsional rigidity was provided by the central chassis tube. There was no rear axle, so you could really get the power down, and it was virtually the same at the rear wheel as it was at the flywheel, and roadholding was outstanding. An Aero Morgan will out-corner a modern Plus 8, and indeed, Charles's own 1,100cc water-cooled JAP Super Sports was able to corner faster than some standard Plus 8s at a recent 'Old Timer' meeting at the Nurburgring. Whilst they would understandably pass him on the straights, he could leave his braking light years later because the three-wheeler is so light, and whip into the corners ahead of them. The car will drift, just like a four-wheeler; the front wheels slide, and the back wheel drifts on power. It is very like racing a single-seater as everything is so direct. Modern motorcycle rubber like Pirelli Phantoms gets good and sticky when it is hot, and this is quite suitable for a three-wheeler Morgan, although of course modern tyres are not eligible in historic racing. Three-wheelers often race with a passenger, like a combination, and the passenger can do some of the work by passing his weight from one side of the car to the other. The ambiance of the experience was summed up by fighter ace Albert Ball, who ordered one of the sporting Grand Prix three-wheelers during the Great War, when he told HFS that 'the merry twinkling of the rocker gear, the odd sparks which fly from the exposed exhaust ports at night, the spots of oil and grease thrown back onto the aero screens; on a bumpy road it's rather like taxiing over a grass aerodrome.'

A couple of years ago the German magazine *Auto Motor und Sport* did a back-to-back test between a BMW Z1 and a Plus 8, and despite the modernity of the German car, the Plus 8 came out on top, chiefly because of its value for money. Charles has thought about a Morgan Plus 12, with an eye on BMW's compact lightweight aluminium V12 unit. The Morgan's long bonnet might well accommodate it. I wonder then why the Plus 4 never got the 2.5-litre straight six engine of the TR6? The BMW angle is pure speculation, as it is too under-developed anyway, but it points out the fertile ground for innovation at Morgan. Other modern concepts such as automatic seatbelts and ABS have been under consideration at some point, and the engines are computerized now. But Charles points out that weight-increasing extras such as ABS may well alienate Morgan customers, many of whom use their cars for competition, and might consider ABS a bit soft. Anyone racing with 3.9-litres would probably want to do their own braking, rather than have the car make up its own mind. 'We like the kind of owner who uses his car in this way,' said Charles. 'The last thing one wants is an owner who buys the car for its looks and posing potential.' The austerity of sports car motoring tends to dissuade such people, who might well be better off in a V12 E-type! A Morgan, he believes, does not need such fripperies as an electronic trip computer. Other manufacturers clearly believe he is right, as the Mazda MX5 is a return to basics, and the Caterham Seven has never compromised.

TROUBLESHOOTER

Many British readers will remember the BBC television series *Troubleshooter*, in which company economics guru and former Chairman of ICI Sir John Harvey-Jones evaluated a number of small companies and suggested ways of improving performance. Five companies were chosen to be in the series, and Morgan was asked specifically if it would participate because the BBC wanted to include a small car manufacturer. Evidently the briefing was inadequate, as Morgan had no idea it was going to be called

Troubleshooter, or that it was to be all about problems.

The Morgan Motor Company was the last in the series, and Sir John declared that new plant and machinery was required to lift production to cope with demand, and also that prices should rise to cut the waiting list and increase profits. Peter and Charles Morgan, whom he criticized for 'touching' diffidence and lack of greed, gave him short shrift on all counts. The ebullient troubleshooter appeared floored. He suggested calling in a manufacturing consultant, and this too was rejected. During the programme, the company announced its plan to raise production from nine cars a week to ten inside a year, a target which they succeeded in achieving.

I include this section because the notorious *Troubleshooter* programme caused such a furore at Morgan, and four years on, everyone at the factory still has something to say about it. Such radical solutions as the programme delivered consolidate and marshall public opinion, and people who knew I was writing a book on Morgan had a view too, so clearly there are things to be said. It had two effects: firstly it concentrated the minds of the cognoscenti as to whether or not Morgan was going about things the right way, at a time of a growth in the specialized market; and it brought the company massive prime-time publicity which resulted in a small flood of orders and a general raising of consciousness about the company. The response to the programme was little short of dramatic. Not only did 90 per cent of commentators agree with the Morgan viewpoint, but the order book was swelled by 400 new commissions in the three months that followed. The attendant interest lasted a lot longer.

It is not just the product that is important to a Morgan customer; it is the whole ethos behind it. Sir John may have grasped the problems at Norton, covered in his

Logging orders for spares in the stores.

subsequent series, rather better than the Morgan situation. Norton, making sophisticated rotary engines for its competent but not outstanding frames, was very top-heavy in a competitive market, and was trying to lead by engineering against the Japanese. The product was good from a technical and practical point of view, but the company was driven financially rather than driven for the product. It would have been better to concentrate on the product and make it at an economic price, rather than compete against the aggressive marketing of the Japanese on their volume basis.

Make no mistake, the flamboyant Sir John Harvey-Jones, moustachioed and tousle-haired, is good television. It is what they describe these days as sexy, meaning the type of programme that seduces the viewers. To show up at Morgan, where legend has it that everything stays much the same, and advocate serious restructuring across the board was certain to grab the

audience's imagination. Sir John is sufficiently charismatic to be lampooned in the satirical magazine *Private Eye*, which has his blustering mannerisms off to a tee. To be fair, Sir John did not want to alter what the cars look like, merely the way they are made. He thought it would be quite easy to double Morgan production without spoiling the product in any way, and that it would be easy for the company to be more efficient, to increase prices and to be more profitable. After the programme he dismissed Peter and Charles's reactions, slating them as having lower ambitions for the company. But it is a family business, and the profit motive is not their uppermost concern. I feel Sir John missed the point. Certainly everyone at Malvern is convinced he competely mis-read Morgan, seeing it like MG at Abingdon perhaps, much more of a mainstream producer than it actually is. He also assumed that Morgan could more or less fool customers that the car was hand-built, get components made outside, and go for a more mass-produced vehicle.

'His thinking all the time was that because it still looked like a Morgan we could get away with it. But you'd never fool genuine Morgan customers like that,' said Sales Director Derek Day. People buy Morgans for precisely the reasons he condemned the company; they want to have a car that is hand-made using traditional tools and materials, that has shuffled in and out of the various workshops; and in general they do not mind waiting because it gives them something to look forward to, and they can save up in the meantime. Sir John did not spend long enough at the factory; you have to be there for days to absorb the nature of the company and its products.

HISTORICAL PRECEDENT

Rather than looking at the factory as a whole, it really has to be regarded as a collection of smaller elements carrying out specialized trades. Although this may seem old-fashioned, it has lots of merits, including flexibility. Looking at the building itself, and the pushing around of the cars from one department to another, many people observe that the order of the production process is illogical. The reason is historical, in that the workshops were built piecemeal as extensions to the original 1919–25 factory and they have hardly changed since. If they did go to the trouble of re-arranging everything in a logical layout it would make very little difference to the running of the company.

The *Troubleshooter* programme was made over the course of a whole year. Works Manager Mark Aston spent six hours with Sir John, talking him through the company philosophy, but, says Mark, 'He'd made his mind up before he came here.' Ultimately, the Morgan Motor Company is not run on a

cost-reduction basis, which should be obvious just looking around. But the beauty of the system is the flexibility and the fact that they can make changes rapidly. There have been occasions in the past where this has happened and extra cars have been built. They do not have the problem of the costs of tooling having to be offset over a long production run. The beauty of Morgan is that it is run to make the product rather than purely to make a profit. And being flexible, they can switch to building more 4/4s, say, if Plus 8 axles are not supplied on time. A while ago when the market was uncertain and there had been an inordinate amount of outgoings, the factory was fired up to produce a few extra cars a week to get them out of trouble.

In the process of any streamlining, some of the skills might be lost. This was one of Sir John's proposals, that Morgan stop making so much of the cars, sub-contract work out, buy in components such as hubs and brakes, and assemble them into the car. This removes not only labour costs but skills too, as well as the responsibility for quality, and taken to its ultimate extreme the factory ends up as an assembly plant. This is the distinction between a hand-built car and a hand-made car. One is assembled by hand, which is very easy and can be done by mechanics and fitters; but Morgans are created by craftsmen, which is a different matter altogether. Most mass-production car factories are really just assembly plants.

SEQUEL REJECTED

Four years on, there was a sequel to see how the 'Troubleshot' companies were faring. Sir John was disappointed not to be invited back to Malvern, as the Morgan programme was quite the most controversial of the first series. Said Peter Morgan, 'We still disagree with Sir John, so there wouldn't have been

It is not just the product that is important to the customer, it is the whole ethos behind it, demonstrated by satisfied customers at the Midland Centre Trial, Pendock.

much point. It might have looked as if we wanted publicity.' As it was, the marque still got a plug in the sequel because the industrial guru met with restorer John Worrall and a Morgan was shown driving along leafy lanes. But he wasted no time in emphasizing the point about an eleven-year waiting list and joked with John Worrall about Heart of England Morgan's notional forty-year waiting list. Sir John proudly announced that despite this, he had bought a Morgan, and produced a Majorette model. Very droll.

Sales Director Derek Day was described as the 'rationer' of Morgans. He is convinced that if they had carried out Sir John's ideas, they would not be in existence today. This contrasts with Sir John's view that if Morgan did nothing, it would, in the course of time, disappear. Yet if the prices of the cars had been doubled and new plant installed, the company might have had a problem in the recession.

The last word should come from Peter Morgan, who has met Sir John Harvey-Jones since the notorious *Troubleshooter* programme. He maintains they are friends. 'But his advice was not correct,' says Peter. 'Although lots of things which he criticized are perfectly valid, his main idea about doubling production and raising prices considerably was wrong; I'll reserve judgement when the five years since the making of the programme are up, but if we'd gone ahead straight away and implemented his recommendations, we'd be in deep trouble by now. Such is the recession we wouldn't have the demand.'

3 Machine Shop

A glance round the parts bins in the machine shop will amaze you. The diversity of components produced here is staggering; items one takes for granted are piled high in their compartments, and parts ranging from king pins and bushes, stub axles and brake drums, shackle pins, various sized nuts and bolts, brake pedals and stone guards, are all machined up and placed in stock, ready to be taken off to be fitted to the cars in chassis assembly. More bins containing the raw material, like drop-forgings for the hubs and brake drums are close by. This is all in one small corner of a workshop containing three lines of lathes. There is no such thing as computerization, robots or machine tools exercising numerical control; the small runs do not justify it in the first place, and in the second, the lathes and drills are kept in excellent working order and regularly serviced. Many of the machines date from the period in the Second World War when the workshop was leased to Standard for machining Spitfire components and munitions.

The machine shop is at the bottom of the hill in the layout of the factory complex. Foreman is Tony Newman, who joined in 1955, making him one of the longest-serving employees at the Morgan Motor Company. When he started, output was six cars a week. Tony has a staff of twenty, including two women, who set their own machines and look after them, a storeman and a labourer, whose job is mainly to clear away the swarf from the lathes. These comprise turret lathes, capstan lathes, which were reconditioned ten years ago, and milling machines. They are huge machines, mostly in their original dark-green paint, turning quite slowly and dribbling frothy green-yellow liquid on their subject to cool it down, as swarf splinters or curls off like orange peel.

They are all virtually as they were when first installed, and until two years ago the tips used to be reground; now they just replace the tip. The machine shop deals with the cast work like brake drums, drop-forgings such as stub axles and wire-wheel hubs. Plus 8 hubs are malleable iron castings and the Plus 4 hub is a drop-forging. When machined, the Plus 8 hub weighs 9lb (4kg) compared with the Plus 4's, which weighs 5lb 8oz (2.5kg). So although the Plus 4's starts off as a very heavy drop-forging, once machined, it is lighter than the casting, and stronger too. Stub axles and hubs are the most difficult components to make because of the fine tolerances on threads. They are sent away to be splined. Painters of Worcester provide most of the castings in aluminium.

It is worth listing the other components produced in the machine shop because it illustrates the diversity of bits which one tends to overlook in a car, and the range of skills needed to make it. On a tour of the lathes, Tony showed me the safety belt mounts, handbrake lever (now 2in (5cm) longer), and its ratchet, oil valve, back brake compensator, master cylinder distance plate, brake caliper brackets, grease caps for the Plus 8 hubs, and spare wheel bracket. These were either being produced or batches had recently been done.

Virtually all brackets are made in-house. There are a number of jigs and 'gadgets' to

Many of the lathes in the machine shop were installed during the Second World War and with regular servicing run as well as ever.

Toolmaker and CAD expert Dave Goodwin making a new bit on the centre-lathe.

Close concentration as a stub axle arm is milled.

Taking the sides off washers so they will fit under the wing.

*Milling the face of a
stub axle.*

*Drilling safety belt
angle-brackets on
the three spindle
drill.*

The spare-wheel carrier is made from rods on a capstan lathe; note the coolant flowing at centre right.

Making the two-seater hood frame.

Parts bins in the machine shop piled high with a multitude of components.

Welding up the chassis frame-front destined for a Plus 8, on a special jig.

The sections for the frame-front are mounted on a special jig which can rotate through 360 degrees.

Machining up Plus 8 wire wheel front hubs on a capstan lathe; note the variety of tools available on the machine which can be swiftly brought into play.

Assembling the stub axle and alloy wheel hub of a Plus 8.

A stock of newly turned wire wheel hubs.

Machine shop foreman Tony Newman joined Morgan in 1955 when output was six cars a week.

make things easier. One is an ingenious saw for cutting steel bars to get the bits to fashion brackets and engine mounts, which are welded up in a side room. Here three blacksmiths carry out the brazing and welding jobs, ranging from frame fronts to engine mounting brackets. Elsewhere someone is soldering the ends on the handbrake cables, others are building up the hub assemblies or making wiper arms. Items made in the forge include side stays, hood frames, bosses for 4/4 water pumps and wing stays. Front suspension damper blades are punched out, and a pile of V8 water pumps wait their turn to be shortened. Once the hood frame is bent, it is stripped down and sent off for powder-coating. This takes place at 100°C, which distorts the metal so the lengths usually have to be re-bent.

So apart from the engine, gearbox and back axle, virtually all the major mechanical componentry is machined up here, by hand, which gives Morgan a huge advantage, because although such items can be sourced outside, the company is assured of a certain quality standard by making these items itself. There is nothing like being self-reliant either.

4 Chassis Assembly Shop

The Morgan chassis is made of Z-section steel, contrary to some expectations that it is of the same wood as the frame. The chassis are made to Morgan specification by ABT at Ross-on-Wye, having been made by Rubery Owen until the late seventies, then Rockwell Thompson until 1992. They arrive at the factory in batches, and it is interesting to spot the 2in (5cm) difference in width and length between the 4/4 and larger Plus 4 and Plus 8 chassis, which will ultimately affect the wheelbase and track of all three models. Some are silver and some are black, because a growing number of customers specify galvanizing, while others are happy to go along with the factory's standard epoxy powder-coating. This involves spray-coating the chassis with resin powder and baking it in an oven. The factory has its own powder-coating booth, where all the small brackets, 'cabs' (or metal fronts) and gearbox covers are treated. The little items are hung like clothes in a long wardrobe and sprayed matt black, then baked in the oven for thirty minutes. Foreman of the chassis assembly shop is David Day, who has worked at Morgan since 1957. He thinks the steel chassis is so substantial that powder-coating is quite adequate, but hot-dip galvanizing can only provide better protection against corrosion. It is an optional extra which has become more and more popular in the last five years.

Smaller items, such as brackets, are hung up in a booth for powder-coating.

GALVANIZING

It is worth describing the process, since roughly half of Morgan's customers are now sufficiently convinced of its merits, but may not be aware of the real advantages and dramas involved. It is named after Luigi Galvani, who made the curious observation that frogs' legs wired to pieces of metal twitched because an electric circuit was completed; the process of galvanizing was patented in 1837 and was generally used for coating mundane household artefacts like bath tubs and milk churns. There are several different methods of galvanizing. Simplest is zinc-rich galvanizing that anyone can do at home with a pot of zinc and a paint brush. At the other end of the scale is zinc-wiping. Car makers like Audi, Fiat and Porsche rely on the zinc-wiping process carried out by the steel producers where the sheet steel is unrolled, treated, then rolled up again. Audi is sufficiently confident of this method to offer a twelve-year guarantee on its products, despite the minimal coating, and the fact that once a panel is cut from the steel sheet, you have a bare ungalvanized edge.

Hot-dip galvanizing, which is how the Morgan chassis are treated, endows the metal with ten times more zinc than the wiping method. The molecular reaction takes place at a very high temperature (450°C), combining the zinc with the surface of the chassis in the dip. It is also said to self-heal any subsequent scratch by means of naturally occurring salts. There is a slight weight increase, amounting to about 11lb (5kg) per chassis, which is really minimal. Hot-dip galvanizing is a spectacular process, carried out at a specialist plant, where the plain mild-steel chassis is first shot blasted, then purified of surface impurities for an hour in hydrochloric acid; it is then coated with flux in a tub of zinc, ammonium chloride and water. Finally it is dunked slowly and carefully in the bath of zinc. Once the cold, damp steel of the chassis contacts the flat calm surface of the molten zinc, all hell breaks loose. The reaction is loud and dramatic, not dissimilar to a miniature volcanic eruption or geyser, accompanied by clouds of steam, chemical

Part of the new intake of major components for a week's work in the chassis assembly shop, comprising five powder-coated and three galvanized chassis, Plus 8 engines from Rover and axles from GKN; bellhousings and metal fronts can be seen at the rear.

Plus 4 chassis takes shape, with Avon Turbospeed-shod chromed wires and front stub-axle and Girling disc brake assembly awaiting fitment.

aromas and strange echoes, the popping and banging of the violent chemical reaction and liquids boiling away. The burned-off flux is skimmed off the surface and the chassis is moved about in the dip to ensure a thorough coating. It is as well to stand clear of the bombardment of flying zinc globules. No matter that hardly anyone but the concours judge will see it, it is nice to know that the galvanized chassis is an attractively spangled silver colour, an effect created by the way the zinc molecules organize themselves, whilst the powder-coated chassis is just plain black.

ASSEMBLY

The chassis assembly shop building is much the same (although the pin-ups on the wall have changed) and the procedure has not varied since 1957 when David Day joined. He recalls making eight cars a week then. He believes ten cars is probably the absolute maximum the current procedure can handle, although very occasionally an extra one is slipped in. A week before a customer's car is ready to be built, the sales office issues a build ticket to the stores, and all departmental foremen get one too, so they know what is up-coming and can order in advance any extra-special options to be built into the car, such as an unusual paint finish or trim detail. Stores then provides an appropriate selection of parts which is laid out, along with engines, axles and wheels, by the waiting chassis in the assembly shop. Cars are assembled on a weekly basis of ten units, and although some components are made in the machine shop, they really start to take shape in the chassis assembly shop. But before assembly can begin there is much preparation to be done.

MODIFYING ENGINES

The larger components are the axles, engines, gearboxes, wheels and tyres, frame fronts, scuttle and valances, and steering column. A number of these major components are received as complete units at the chassis assembly shop, including the engines. The Rover engines then have to be modified to enable them to fit and run in the Morgan chassis. The T16 unit comes separate from its gearbox, which necessitates modifications being made to the chassis cross-member, bellhousing and bulkhead; a backplate is sourced from the Sherpa van

parts bin. The clutch housing has to be modified too, but otherwise it is a straightforward installation.

The Plus 8 unit is particularly difficult, as it has to have its water pump cut off. It is too long as it is, and it has to be grafted back on the side of the engine; normally the water pump has a shaft onto which the fan screws, and this is ground off. An electric fan on the other side of the radiator takes its place. There are major alterations to the clutch housing, which projects in an inappropriate place for one of the chassis cross-members. This has to be removed and the housing sent away and welded up, and the slave cylinder is moved to the top of the bellhousing. All relatively major stuff, which has to be carried out before the engine can be fitted. Manifolds too are changed, the T16 having a particularly attractive four-branch system, and the engines are then mated with their gearboxes. The mountings themselves are fitted, and the harness, starter motor and other ancilliaries are attached. The Ford units for the 4/4 are more straightforward, and they come in unit with the Sierra gearbox mated to the backplate, having been

A consignment of 1,796cc Ford Zeta engines and gearboxes waiting installation in the 4/4s; note the relatively tall fuel-injection system.

specially modified by Powrtorque to suit the Morgan.

The brake drums are made at Morgan, and then sent to GKN for installation in the rear axle assembly. The axles, formerly Salisbury, are made by GKN to Morgan specification, and each model has a different axle. The final drive ratios are different, and like the chassis, the 4/4 axle is narrower than that of the identical Plus 4 and Plus 8. They are then dispatched to Malvern. Back at base then, the axles are painstakingly fitted with springs, shackles, the handbrake cable, rear shock absorber mountings, and brake rod yokes. They are then ready to be installed in the chassis. Next, a week's supply of appropriate wheels and tyres is made up. These correspond to the three different models and their relative wire or steel option. Generally the Plus 8 gets 205VR/60–15 Pirelli P600s, the Plus 4 195/60–R15 Avon Turbospeeds, and the 4/4 runs on relatively high-profile 175 HR–15 Uniroyals.

The 'cab', (also known as the metal front or scuttle) and valances, front cowl box, toolbox, and steering box covers are all made in the sheet metal shop, and a ready powder-coated stock is laid in at the chassis assembly shop. Frame-fronts are welded up in the machine shop. To start with, the scuttle is drilled to take the collapsible steering column. The toolbox and clutch reservoir are attached, the valances drilled to accommodate brake pipes and hoses and the radiator mounting bar. These panels are now ready for fitting, and the build can commence.

ASSEMBLING THE RUNNING GEAR

Every Thursday, ten chassis arrive at the chassis assembly shop, delivered somewhat agriculturally on a fork-lift. They are laid out on pairs of trestles, and preparation takes place so the chassis can receive the running gear. The layout of the chassis itself has changed very little over the years, apart from being widened, lengthened and strengthened for the Plus 8 back in 1969 and 1976. It resembles the flattened skeleton of a small boat with three transoms. These boxed or sometimes tubular cross-members move around for the various different engine and gearbox mountings, but structurally it has not really altered. It is first checked for quality, flatness and alignment. But drilling it for engine mountings, pedals, rear axle, frame-front and so on is crucial, and jigs and templates are used, left and right hand. This process takes two days, and, says Dave Day, 'It's not as simple as people think, screwing a few nuts and bolts together. There are lots of problems to be overcome in preparing the chassis.' So it is not until the Monday that chassis are moved across from one side of the workshop to the other, to lie in a row on trestles beneath the travelling pulley system, when Dave Day and his team of four fitters set to and assembly proper commences.

The fitting order never varies. The floor, made of exterior-grade marine plywood, supplied ready creosoted by the wood shop, is laid down in the chassis, together with the deal-pine tank board; a softer wood is used so the fuel tank can bed down more snugly, and the tank is protected from stone chips. Of mechanical parts, the phallic fly-off handbrake goes on first, then the pedal assembly, the brake master cylinder, and the rear suspension roll bar. Everything is done methodically but swiftly. Blink, or go off to the machine for a coffee, and you miss something.

On go the exhaust pipe mountings, the brake pipes, and the axle rebound rubbers. The triangulated frame-front, a product of the machine shop's welding department, is fitted. This carries the front suspension, and the 4/4 and Plus 4 frame-fronts are 2in (5cm) narrower than the Plus 8's. With the wheels

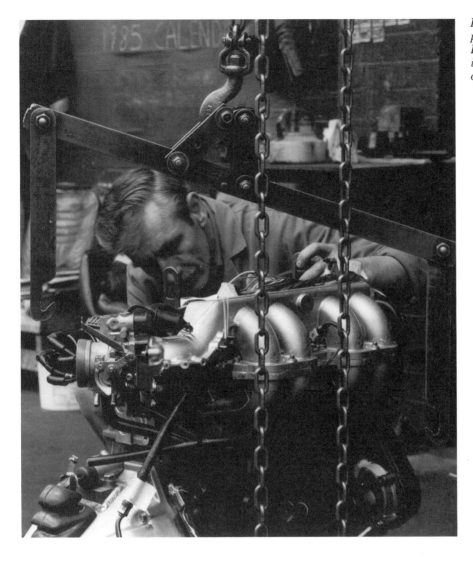

Foreman Dave Day prepares to hoist a Rover T16 engine into its Plus 4 chassis.

on the Plus 4 wire wheel track measures 58in (1,473mm) front, 63in (1,600mm) rear, whilst the Plus 8 on alloys measures 61in (1,549mm) front and 63in (1,600mm) rear; but the track of a Plus 8 on wire wheels measures 63in (1,600mm) front and 65in (1,651mm) rear.

Pre-formed brake pipes go in at the front of the chassis, and then the engine and gearbox is hoisted in place by chains descending from the hand-hauled overhead pulley system. It is logical to get the engine in at this stage because of ease of access to the bare chassis, and the importance of alignment of moving mechanical components. And also because there is no danger of damaging paint or panel work at a later stage.

The axle is built up as a unit with the leaf springs (five a side as standard), then lifted into place by hand by two men. It is secured to the chassis by four bolts in spring hangers.

The prop-shaft universal joint is mated with the Plus 8 gearbox.

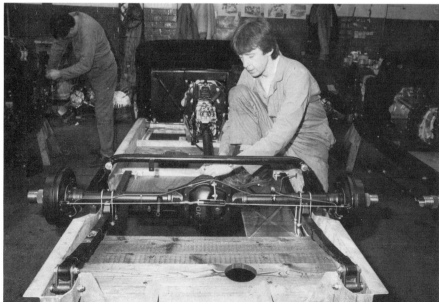

A degree of physical contortion is needed to bolt the prop-shaft universal joint to the final drive unit.

At this point the brakes are checked and adjusted. The pipes, compensator and brake rods are connected to the rear drums, and the handbrake cable is fitted and adjusted up. Next it is the turn of the rear telescopic dampers, and then the prop-shaft, before the panel work goes on to clad the front of the chassis. The scuttle is fitted with a jig in order to achieve the correct angle for mounting the wood frame. The valances too are aligned with jigs before being bolted in place. These take the radiator mounting bar brackets and the front cowl box. Cars for the US market have louvres at the trailing edge.

Morgan relied on a Burman cam-and-peg steering system until 1985, and when Burman stopped production, the Plus 8 went to a Jack Knight rack-and-pinion system, and the Plus 4 and 4/4 used the French-made Gemmer recirculating ball steering box. This is actually just a better quality version of the earlier Burman system, giving a lighter feel with self-centring. Rack-and-pinion has been optional in the Plus 4 since 1991. The 4/4 and Plus 4 chassis are jig-drilled

to receive the steering box, while the Plus 8's steering rack is mounted on the frame-front. Using a universal coupling, the collapsible extruded mesh AC Delco steering column is then jigged into position and the assembly bolted up.

FRONT SUSPENSION

Stub axles are received from the machine shop as sub-assemblies, coming complete with discs, hubs, calipers, king pins and bushes, plus attendant lube-bolt, damper bronze aluminium block, and damper blade. They are mounted in the chassis, clad within the main coil springs and the rebound springs, together with the steering dampers, and bolted into position. Morgan front suspension may be considered idiosyncratic these days, because it has altered little in character since 1911. The principle is that the long king pins slide through a pair of phospher-bronze bushes, which being soft metal, are prone to wear within 15–20,000

A row of chassis in an advanced state of completion with steering and front suspension still to assemble. The four nearest are Plus 8s, the rest Plus 4s, and four are galvanized.

*The AC Delco
collapsible steering
column is fitted to
a left-hand drive
Plus 4.*

miles (24–32,000 kilometres). They then
need replacing because the resulting play in
the front wheels will cause the car to wander. Having said that, some people have
never had to change them. As a precaution,

the bushes can be greased fortnightly, or
lubricated when in motion by Morgan's own
curious 'one-shot' system which (since 1950)
allows the driver to press a button on the
transmission tunnel and drip engine oil

*Tightening the king
pin lube bolt, which
connects with the
'one-shot'
lubrication system
and will ultimately
lubricate the king
pin and bushes;
shock absorbers and
damper blades have
yet to be fitted.*

Plus 8 chassis takes shape; AC Delco collapsible steering column can be seen linking with Jack Knight rack-and-pinion system; front brakes are dual circuit Girling discs.

down the king pin. The damper lube system is done away with for racing, but one wonders why a steel pipe is used when plastic would be rather simpler to install.

Whilst the 4/4 and Plus 4 share the same suspension componentry, the Plus 8 has chunkier stub axles, and the coil springs at the front are thicker and one coil shorter than the other models'. The forward mounting points for the rear leaf springs are 2.5in (6.25cm) lower, so the springs have a tilt to them, and there is a slightly larger dip in

Front hub assembly grows, and foreman Dave Day's next job here will be to link the stub axle with track rod end and telescopic damper.

The chassis, complete with powertrain, is pushed outside by three men and rolled at considerable speed down the slope to the wood shop, and woe betide anyone who gets in the way!

the chassis rails under the axle to allow more clearance for rebound.

Next, the track rod assemblies are fitted, plus the Armstrong telescopic shock absorbers. The steering dampers are attached to the chassis and the front brake hoses connected up. Now that the steering is connected to the stub axles, it can be set and adjusted. The brake and clutch reservoirs are filled with fluid, and then are bled, and the engine and gearbox filled with oil. The wheels are fitted and, using jacks, the rolling chassis is dropped off the trestles for the final tracking and alignment. One or two cars may have got left behind because of a parts shortage; three cars had yet to receive their rear axles during one of my visits, although everything else had been fitted to their chassis.

By now it is Wednesday afternoon, and following a cross-check inspection by final assembly foreman Don Passey, the build ticket with the customer's name and specifications is attached, and ten more cars are on their way to the wood shop to have their frames fitted. This event is at first alarming to behold. A mule steering-wheel is fitted

temporarily. Then each one is wheeled outside onto the factory access road by three men, then one leaps aboard and the car whistles down the slope, gathering momentum with the gradient, and is steered at an indecent pace into the wood shop where the standing 'driver' brings it to rest with the handbrake.

Anything stripped down to its bare essentials has a sporting look about it, and at this stage the Morgan rolling chassis look like nothing so much as a team of pre-war formula racing cars. Keeping track of what goes on in the chassis assembly shop is more difficult than anywhere else in the factory, because of the myriad small parts and variety of jobs to be done fettling the chassis. It has been said that although the cars might look identical, there will inevitably be minute differences between each one because everything is hand-made. This is a bit of a myth, because tolerances are actually very tight at every stage of the build process, from stub axles and steering to rear axle and brakes. It is only at the paint and trim stage that every car becomes different.

5 Wood Shop

Why ash? Its traditional uses were in the spokes of agricultural cart and carriage-wheel manufacture, axe and other tool-handles, then tennis rackets and other sports equipment, such as fishermen's landing net handles, walking sticks and billiard cues. It is used by cabinet-makers, vehicle coachbuilders, and for oars, tillers and canoe frames by boat-builders. As a hardwood, *Fraxinus excelsior* is inherently strong, although I remember vividly my zany art master beating the whole class with billiard cues and ending up with a lot of broken wood and not much pain inflicted! However, having seen a Morgan's undamaged ash frame, bowed but unbroken after a two-ton side impact test, I would have few qualms about the ability of the car to withstand an unwanted side entry. In another crash test, the chassis was bent but, incredibly, the frame was unharmed.

Morgans have always been built with a traditional ash frame, because one of the beneficial properties of ash is its flexibility, unlike oak or mahogany. Like beech, ash will flex a little and then resume its original shape, but it is tougher than beech, and indeed any other home-grown hardwood. Under the same circumstances of duress, oak will just crack and splinter. Ash is used for hammer handles because it is resilient; an oak handle would shatter. Young fast-grown ash has properties of strength, toughness and flexibility, if not natural durability. North American hickory is slightly tougher, and is used for such things as pick-axe

General view of the wood shop as a row of Plus 8s have their frames built.

handles. Teak has similar flexible properties to ash, which is why it is used in boat manufacture, but it is an oily wood and therefore too messy for the car body frame. Also its oilyness precludes preservative. Although it is not native, teak may be cheaper than ash, but the stoppages caused by saw cleaning outweigh any other advantages over ash. Machining properties of ash are good, which is important.

The trees used by Morgan mostly grow in Scotland, although there may be a return to a source in Belgium (there were problems with wartime shrapnel embedded in Belgian trees), and the main supplier is based in Liverpool. Unlike coppiced ash, which grows fast in a packed woodland situation, the trees are always mature, over 100 years old and up to 60ft (18m) tall before they are felled. The wood has to be carefully selected, and the cut planks batched according to which section of the frame the wood is destined for, as the grain must run in the right direction. The outer section of the mature trunk tends to be brittle, so only the fast-growing heart-wood is used. This requires a degree of skill on the part of the woodyard sawing up the trees, and the sawn-up trunks are then dispatched to Malvern. Here they lie as planks, carefully separated one from another by fillets of wood to allow air to circulate, and they are left to season for at least a year in the open wood shed at the factory. Although the wood is kiln dried before Morgan receives it, there is still a quantity of sap which has to dry out.

SAW MILL

There is a small mill, adjoining but closed off from the wood shop, just across the factory access road from the wood shed, which receives the planks, and the foreman of the wood shop, Graham Hall, carefully selects the pieces he will use in frame manufacture. From time to time he will reject part of a consignment, but reflects that 'We can't tell the trees how to grow! We have to take what comes to a certain extent, but we do try to

Basic cuts are first made in the saw mill, machined up on a band saw in batches of forty or fifty.

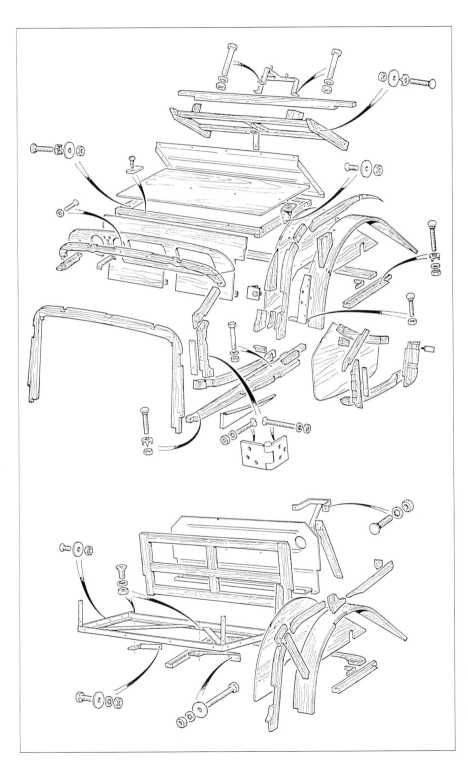

Exploded view of the individual parts that make up the ash frame. The lower illustration shows the rear section of a four seater.

keep out the knots.' A veteran of forty years with Morgan, Graham does not actually have to visit the forests, as Morgan relies on its two timber merchants to select a good grade of timber.

Accompanied by a strong smell of freshly cut wood and sawdust, planks are cut into progressively smaller chunks by the heavy duty dimension saw in the mill, then planed up to get closer to usable lengths. Graham will then decide what parts are to be made out of which piece of wood. There are 94 different sections of body rail making up the two-seater frame, and 114 in the four-seater frame, so the task of selection is by no means straightforward. Some of the sections have compound curves carved out of them, so there must be absolutely no soft sap-wood. The machine operators in the mill are careful to exclude all but the best of the grain. The sections are made in batches of forty or fifty, so that the saws, routers and planing machinery can be set up to do one job at a time. For instance, a day may be spent making bottom door rails or door fronts, and the next day it might be the dash rail or elbow rail. The stocks are made at a similar rate to the production of the cars themselves. Sophisticated laser cutters exist which could make the relevant three-dimensional cuts in one go and thus speed up the process, but for the time being, the machinery would not be out of place in a rural furniture-maker's workshop. Charles Morgan speculates about updating some of the machinery, for the spindle moulder is over fifty years old; a CNC router would be more efficient, for example, but it seems to me that the pace of the wood-section manufacture matched the car production admirably. Computerized machinery would seem rather out of place, and everything used at present is in perfect working order in any case. To update machinery in one workshop would mean doing the same right throughout the factory. It would not make any sense

at all for Morgan to replace its craftsmen with automated machinery when the customer is buying exactly those skills; and besides, over-investment in new plant in a recession in order to supply a small niche market would not be prudent either.

JIGS

The final cuts are all made on the spindle moulder, with the section of wood offered up to it by hand in a jig or template. Some of the sections are quite complicated, curving in two directions at the same time, like the upper and lower door rails. The curves are cut into the piece of wood rather than bending it, which would be very time consuming. The jigs are made up of two plywood plates with grab handles which are held by the operator, and the section of wood to be cut is sandwiched between them. Using the grab handles the jigs are placed down on the flat steel plate beside the double-headed spindle router, which then cuts up to the edge of the plywood template. Before these jigs came into use, the wood section was hand-held, which was extraordinarily dangerous for fingers. The jig is pressed to the tip of the router to obtain the correct profile. There may be at least two jigs involved in the shaping of a piece of wood, depending on the dimensions and curvature of the rail. There are no less than seven jigs for making the door rocker rail because of its multifarious bends and facets. So when one side of the section has been shaped, the jig can be reversed for doing the opposite side, and the jigs are swapped over to cut the other dimensions. The cut is sufficiently smooth as to require no planing, and the jigs ensure a stock of identical pieces ready to be used in the frame. A gauge of the jigs' accuracy is a cross-frame check at the end of assembly; if there is a discrepancy of 2mm, the frame is considered to be not up to scratch and is

junked, and this rarely happens for the system could not tolerate such wastage. So the production method is remarkably efficient considering the frame is six feet long.

Having joined Morgan in 1953, Graham Hall remembers the current Production Manager coming into the wood shop to play and being chased around by the men! Mrs Hall works in the trim shop, and their son Nigel is one of the coachbuilding team in the wood shop. Obviously Graham knows the frame making process inside out. It has altered quite significantly over the years, with subtle improvements to increase the strength. Graham has been closely involved in the frame's evolution, and is concentrating on developments like the incorporation of side-impact strengtheners in the doors, and this was being experimented with in the development shop while I was at the factory. The back end of the four-seater frame has just been re-shaped to allow more space in the rear of the car. The other innovation, seen as a prototype at the 1992 Motor Fair, is the making and fitting of longer doors to make it easier to get in and out, particularly in the four-seater cars. As we talked, Graham was making up the relevant jigs for the

Basic shape for the door rocker is sawn from a block of ash on a band saw.

spindle moulder, as they would naturally be different for a new longer door size and correspondingly shorter elbow and door-shut rail. Jigs have a finite life, and replacing them is an ongoing process. He had just finished making new jigs for the rocker panel, and the new sections will be a little thicker than the old ones. Getting the jigs right is vital, and armed with ruler, dividers and compass, Graham takes his time over

Cutting the piece for the door rocker on the spindle moulder. No less than seven jigs are required for this section because of its various facets.

this, since the jig has to be spot on and repeat itself every time. Jigs can take about a week to make.

FRAME ASSEMBLY

A stock of rails and wheelarches is always ready for the week's production in hand. Using jigs for accuracy, the basic frames are assembled in two halves, front and back, which are then joined together and checked with jigs again. Each frame is the responsibility of one man, working on a bench over on one side of the workshop, and there are four coachbuilders involved in assembly. They tend to work in batches of six at a time, endeavouring to finish a batch before the weekend break and thus avoid warping. Hand tools are used in assembly of the frame, from clamps and planes to ratchet screwdrivers and drills. Drills are almost always electric, but power screwdrivers are not much in evidence; they do have them,

cordless battery-powered Hitachi models, and one charge lasts all day. The problem is that they are torqued up to a particular setting with a consequent loss of sensitivity; it is necessary to check the fixing by hand afterwards, so they are seldom used. Power tools do not actually save much time, so expert are the craftsmen with their regular equipment.

Each two-seater body takes between ten and eleven hours to assemble, and a four-seater between twelve and fourteen hours. 4/4 frames are smaller than Plus 4 and Plus 8, and four-seaters are different again, being taller in 4/4 format than Plus 4 unless specified as a Plus 4 body. The sections for the frame rails are screwed and glued together with a PVC waterproof glue, which is not broken down by the Cuprisol. This noxious preservative will break down some adhesives. Ash is actually quite resistant to preservative treatment. The PVC glue comes in gallon drums, and is decanted into smaller Evo-stick or washing-up liquid containers

Frames are assembled in two halves, which are then joined together using greased brass screws.

The scuttle rail and dashboard rail form the top front of the frame; triangular supports hold the front half in position until it is secured to the back half.

for ease of handling. Before the days of PVC glue, the assembly was done using a fish glue, which was applied to the joint with a brush. It consisted of rendered down cows' hooves, which consolidated when not in use and had to be melted over a gas ring. I remember using it when making picture frames during school holidays. It smelt quite sickly and gave an entirely different dimension to the concept of glue sniffing.

All joints are clamped up while the glue dries to make them good and tight, and there is much care and extra planing to ensure all wooden surfaces are perfectly smooth. Remarkable, considering few owners will ever see the frame, but it provides an ideal basis for the panelling which will follow, and is an example of the factory's high production standards.

Each section of the frame has a special name. Foremost is the scuttle rail, running in a hoop from one side of the car to the other. Attached to this is the dashboard rail which projects backwards to take the facia board; the hinge-piece is ahead of the doors, butting into the dash rail and curved rockers just beneath the doors. The sill boards are just underneath them. Behind the door apertures are the elbow rails, joined by the rear wheelarch sides and wheelarch bends; the back end of the frame is made up of the top back rail, inside frame, and the spare-wheel frame, and finally the rear bottom rail. There are noggin braces at crucial points such as between the rear wheelarch rails and sides, and the four-seater frame is obviously more squared off and braced accordingly. Its elbow rails and door pillars are a different shape as well. There is a separate inside frame on which a saddle board is dropped to cover the axle. If anything the four-seaters are easier to make, being almost square frames at the rear. In general the curved elbow rails are probably the most difficult to assemble; the hinge pillar has a joint in the top corner which has to be good as it supports the weight of the door.

The rear wheelarches are made of three separate lengths of ash, glued together and bent to the appropriate curvature in these clamps, and then cured for six to eight hours.

REAR WHEELARCH CLAMPS

The rear wheelarches are made of three six-foot lengths of ash, each one 0.25in (0.6cm) thick and 9in (23cm) wide, bonded together with the same two-compound beetle cement adhesive that has always been used, and is typical of wooden aircraft construction. It dries incredibly hard. The glued-up ash strips are placed in curved clamps constructed of hefty wooden blocks, which correspond

Screwing the inner wheelarch panel onto the bent rear wheelarch. Templates for dashboards can be seen hanging on the back wall.

Plus 8 rear end shows deal tank board and spare wheel frame; rear wheelarches have been cut to taper to the bottom rail.

to the required shape of the rear wheelarch. The clamps are then wheeled into a curing oven where they set over six to eight hours in the correct shape. They are battened up to ensure they stay in that shape, as the ideal curing time in the clamp would be twenty-four hours. With the loss of Saturday morning overtime working in 1990, there has been a need to accelerate the process slightly to compensate for the five-day week. There are three clamps, one dating from 1947 and two from 1963; and they look even older. The resulting laminated ash strips of the rear wheelarches are amply strong enough to take the seatbelt mountings, and in fact the entire car can be hoisted up by them. The inner wheelarch is formed of marine ply, being less porous, resilient, and simply a convenient way of spanning a flat space. These are screwed to the bent wheelarch ply when it emerges from the kiln clamps. Eventually they will be protected by a coat of

underseal. The floorboards, which went in right at the beginning, are exterior-use birch ply, and, like the pine tank boards, are liberally creosoted for about six hours.

PRESERVATIVE

You can smell the destination of the frame's next phase as you walk round the factory exterior. When it has been glued and screwed together, the frame is taken back outside the wood shop to a dipping tank in a well-ventilated hut behind the wood shed. It is attached to a pulley and lowered into the tank, where it is immersed for at least three hours in (Lindane free) Cuprisol 'T' wood preservative. Frames made at the end of the day spend the whole night in the dull green fluid, and the chemical thus impregnates the entire grain of the thickest pieces of wood. After the preservative treatment, the

A newly made frame drains after being soaked in the dipping tank; since 1986, frames have been steeped in Cuprisol for several hours, and some overnight; the dark green fluid turns the ash a pale khaki colour.

frames are brought back in to be fitted to the rolling chassis. Having arrived from the chassis assembly shop, these are lifted up with trolley jacks and placed on trestles again for the fitting. It takes two men to lift a frame onto the chassis, then one person takes over, first applying a mastic damp course between metal and wood. Then a 1in wide by 0.125in (25 × 3mm) thick white Bostick sealing strip is laid on the mastic, with yet another layer of mastic sealant on top of the sealing strip, which extends around the bulkhead. It has not always been so thorough a job, waterproofing having

Two men match the frame up to its chassis; it will be secured in place with ten stainless steel coach bolts.

This shows the detailed joinery of the four-seater frame, and is one of the first of the frames made 2in wider. There are 114 different sections of wood in a four-seater frame.

been previously a simple black Bostik no. 3 adhesive. The damp course applied, two men lift the frame onto the chassis, where it is lined up exactly. The frame is pushed up hard against the bulkhead by inserting wedges between the rear axle and the wheelarch and levering it up. Then it gets clamped in place. Nuts, bolts and screws are zinc plated and passivated; five stainless steel coach bolts a side are used to secure the frame to the chassis, bolting through between wood and steel. Thirty-two screws secure the frame to the steel bulkhead, and the holes are drilled by practised eye. If the customer's order includes a scuttle roll bar, it is fitted here, using high-tensile bolts. This steel hoop helps stiffen the whole car at scuttle level, and is also a protective device.

Some frames fitted and waiting for doors, whilst a couple are stacked up to save space.

A separate plate is required behind the hinge rail if the roll bar is fitted.

Whilst the frame takes shape someone else is making a stock of seat squabs and backs for two- and four-seaters, and these go directly to the trimmers to be upholstered. The doors are made specifically for each frame, and for each side of the body, and as you would expect, all the joints are cut and assembled by hand. There can be a 0.0625in (1.5mm) variation between them, and whilst great care is taken, measuring constantly, it is impossible to be absolutely spot-on every time. Gaps round the door frames are set to an exact measurement, and they are chocked in position while the stainless steel hinges are screwed in place. The frame is of course an integral structure in its own right, and over the years, it has been altered where weaknesses have shown up in accidents or through rotting and decay, so that today's cars are inevitably stronger than earlier 4/4s

Planing up a door frame.

Nigel Hall drills holes in the door frame for location of the catch and handle.

and Plus 4s. The wood shop plays a part in the restoration of old Morgans, where new sections of frame, or even complete frames are required, and the pattern may have changed slightly. The old one can be recreated, which may be difficult, depending on the age of car, or the customer can update his car, especially if it is to be repanelled.

No alteration is made without a great deal of thought, because to change one set of jigs often means changing several more so that sections marry up correctly. There is a great deal of strength in the wood itself, and a Morgan frame used to be reckoned to have a life-span of perhaps ten years before attention was required, even twenty years if the

Fitting the door frame; gaps are measured precisely and monitored frequently during fitting to be sure they are constant. Note the wearing of safety glasses.

car was used in a dry climate. Until 1983, the factory's single precaution was to paint the frame black. But untreated with wood preservative, it can succumb relatively quickly to damp and the rigours of hood-down all-weather motoring. One of the factors causing damp to attack the wood is moisture retention in the upholstery, although leather breathes better than synthetic materials. Good ventilation then, is essential. Most prone to failure through damp was the sill board under the door, the door rocker itself and the scuttle down-rail. Fortunately these sections could be replaced without having to go in for a serious rebuild. One of the advantages of Morgan ownership is that the car can be dismantled relatively easily and restored when necessary, and components are available from the factory for all models going back to the early 1950s.

Most Morgan restorers obtain their parts direct from the factory, although anything pre-1950 would need to be specially made. As we shall see, the factory does undertake restorations, but firms like Melvyn Rutter, Black Phey and Heart of England Morgans have the facilities at hand to make their own frames and machine new parts. The three-wheeler club stocks re-manufactured parts.

Since 1984, Morgan frames have received the Cuprisol treatment, which effectively protects the ash hardwood from wet and dry rot and inhibits any bugs which might fancy a free ride. These may be a real problem in Africa. The product is Cuprisol rather than Cuprinol, the distinction being that the PCPs are absent in the former. It gives the frame a greenish-grey hue, and the rather lovely grain of the ash is still clearly visible, unlike in the pre-Cuprisol days of black paint.

It is easy to criticize a pre-preservative wooden frame which lasted twenty years as being a short-lived affair, but few owners of steel-bodied cars in the 1950s and 1960s expected their cars would last that long; besides which obsolescence meant replacement long before the twenty years was up. The ash frame has many advantages over one in aluminium or steel, in that it will not corrode, rust or fatigue. If a vehicle built with an ash frame is looked after, it will endure indefinitely. The beauty of the Morgan frame is that once dismantled, a new section can be screwed and glued in where necessary, and the Cuprisol ensures the frame is more durable even if the car is not looked after.

6 Sheet Metal Shop

Coming back up the hill by one workshop is the sheet metal shop, known affectionately as the 'tin shop'. The cars, now sporting their wooden frames, are pushed up from the wood shop and enter the next phase of their build programme. And that's not the only programme on the go, for pop music, played loud but at tolerable volume elsewhere, is dished out at mega-decibels as that's the only way it can be heard above the deafening and incessant clamour of hammers on metal. What a racket! Thor's caverns can never have been like this. It is by far the noisiest of the factory workshops, and quite reasonably most people wear ear defenders or ear plugs. If you need to talk to someone, it is best to wait for the hallowed teabreak when all is quiet.

It is here that the nature of the end product becomes clear, because the panelling includes the distinctive wings and cowl. The material may be either steel or aluminium, or a mixture of the two; side panels and rear panels are invariably aluminium, and cowl, scuttle and valances are always in steel for greater strength and rigidity. The Morgan is a long car in relation to its width, and by virtue of its build, there is a lot of movement in the body, so the main structural elements have to be resistant to too much movement. Valances help support the weight of the wings for example. For the body, the customer may choose between steel and aluminium. According to foreman Geoff Brewer, the ratio is now 60:40 in favour of aluminium bodies, despite the extra cost. Most people who order aluminium are doing so because it is far lighter; there is a weight saving of 88lb (40kg) on a car built entirely with steel panels. It is no easier to work with than steel, apart from the weight factor, which Geoff thinks makes an aluminium-bodied car more enjoyable to produce than a steel car, from the craftsman's point of view at least. Sometimes an aluminium body is specified with steel wings, which may afford greater protection against minor scrapes. A steel car will be perhaps the more resilient if it is to be used every day, but since the lighter aluminium is available, surely this is the material to go for; all great coachbuilt sports cars should be clad in aluminium. It has the distinct advantage of being less prone to corrosion, although steel and aluminium together are notoriously bad neighbours in this respect. Morgan uses 18-gauge steel and 16-gauge aluminium, which is quite thick yet relatively easy to work.

Every panel starts off as a flat sheet of steel or aluminium and, working a week ahead of the cars in build, the sheets are marked out with a template, and with a few exceptions of detail work done on the guillotine, they are cut out using simple hand-held universal snips and straight shears. Hand-held electric cutters are used for some bigger jobs. The 'tin gods' who work in sheet metal all have their own sets of tools, comprising a variety of hammers and mallets, scribers, hacksaws and snips. A selection of wooden (beech) blocks is available for bending the metal over to create curves or angles. The patterns they use all hang on the workshop walls, to be taken down and used when needed. Once they have been cut out, the precise shape of the panels has to be defined, with reference to the particular car they are

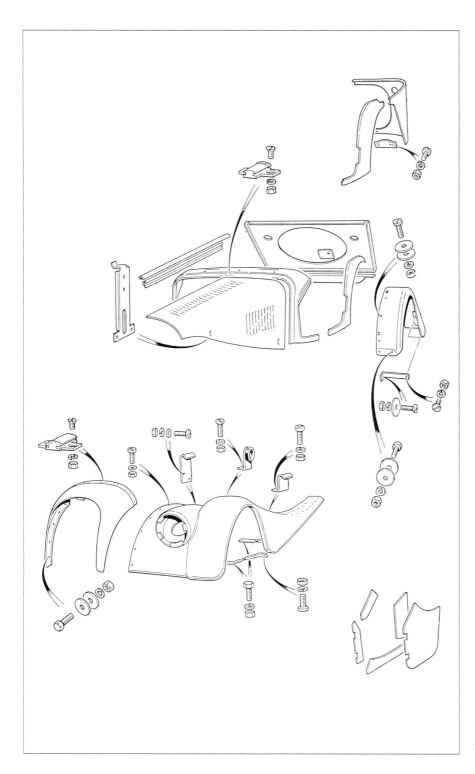

The aluminium (or steel) parts of the Morgan frame. The cowl and scuttle are always in steel. The four seater rear panel section is shown at top right.

Rare use of a power tool; hand-held electric shears are used when making a long straight cut.

Smaller cuts are made with universal snips or straight shears, such as on this rear panel.

destined for. The edges are all turned over by 0.25in (6mm) at a right-angle to start with, to provide an edge to tack the panel onto the corresponding wooden rail of the frame. The edge is then doubled-up flat against the frame, and in this way, the fixing is hidden from the outside, and the panel rim is also strengthened and provided with a good finish. A couple of quaint machines on the end of a bench and which look like mincers, are called the Spinning Jenny and swaging machine. These veterans of fifty years are used for turning the edges, which are polished off with a round-edged hand-held block. The methods have not changed and the tools have not altered. The

workshop walls are tidier, but otherwise the environment is the same as it was forty years ago. Only the cars have evolved. The car you get is unique, but the downside is that if a panel is damaged in some way, a replacement will have to be specially made for it, and that might involve replacing the panels which butt up to it; a new front wing may mean a new bonnet to match its fit.

At the same time, restoration work has to be fitted in, often for the older models. A pre-1954 car may have to have new flat-radiator style panels specially made for it, including the rad itself. Other panels are regularly made for stores, which are to fulfil outside orders, probably from an agent or restorer.

One of the 'tin gods' deftly hammering over a leading edge, which is the best way of finishing a free piece of metal.

PANELLING THE FRAME

The week's running order begins with the fabrication of detail work, with items made up on a continuous bench along one side of the workshop. These include the scuttle panels, frame-fronts and valances fitted earlier on by the chassis assembly shop. Then there are toolboxes and gearbox covers to be made, and these have strengthening shapes rolled into them. For instance, before the gearbox cover has its component panels welded together, each part is embossed with a line which makes it stiffer. The centre section of the car is panelled first, which

takes two days per car to accomplish. On go the side panels, followed by the scuttle panel, then the doors are clad. The wire beading which forms the all-important weather strip diagonally down either side of the scuttle is slowly soldered on. In practice this throws rain water away from the door panel gap when the car is in motion. Then the rear-threequarter and rear panels are tacked on.

Wings are fitted next, for which the cars are shunted up to the far end of the workshop to be mated with their mudguards. These are the only body sections to be made elsewhere, due to the absence of rollers big enough to create their distinctive contours. Since the 1950s they have been made by Eva Brothers of Crabtree Lane, Clayton, Manchester, where there are massive rollers for turning truck mudguards. Morgan wings front and back have complex curves and require similar rollers to create them, compounded by the fact that Plus 8 wings have grown progressively wider. By the time this is published, questions of wing quality will doubtless have been answered. From time to time there have been lapses involving the welded join between the round nascelles for the lights and the wing, which has resulted in too much filler having to be used. Front cowls are attached next, and the winging and cowling will have taken a day and a half.

Meanwhile, the bonnet sides are being prepared. These start off as single flat sheets, measuring 84in × 44in (213 × 118cm), which is divided in two. Each half is fed by two of the three bonnet-makers into what is best described as a mangle. This device was in use during the mid-twenties, and still performs an invaluable service. One person holds the metal steady while the other turns a handle, and the plate progresses halfway through the mangle and gets a curve put in it. This should be exactly right for the curvature of the Morgan bonnet, but

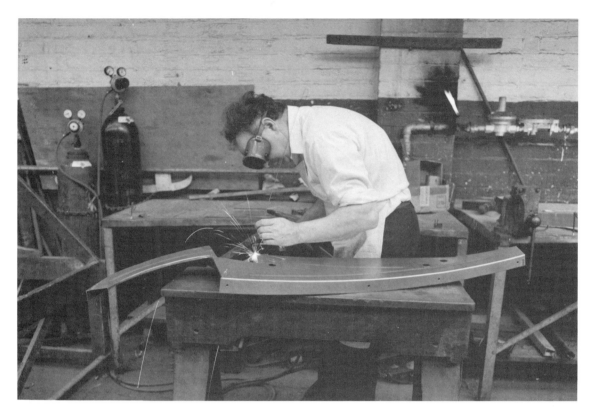

Finishing off a valance; note the panel's strengthening lines and gentle curvature.

Welding up the sides of the scuttle or metal front using an oxyacetylene torch and spelter.

Making final adjustments to the rear tonneau deck before fitting.

if it isn't, it is taken over to a well-worn section of beech trunk not much smaller in diameter than a telegraph pole, and the curve is increased by manipulating the metal over the wood. After every stage in its manufacture, each bonnet half is offered up to the car to make sure it will fit. The top edges are bent over in a tight loop which will later house the hinges. These will be spot-welded in position. Then the side edges are turned over a length of wire, the best way of finishing the edge of a free piece of metal.

The rear threequarter panel is clad in aluminium.

113

Soldering the weather bead down the front of the door.

Side edges of the wing are skilfully turned over to provide a lip for fitting.

Care is needed when fixing the front wings to the frame to avoid sagging.

The Plus 8 sits on trestles whilst the wing is attached.

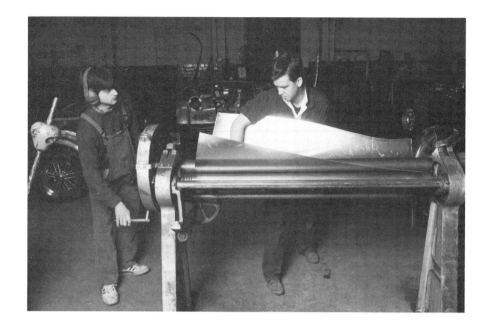

The bonnet halves are bent in a mangle; this machine was installed in the 1920s.

When the men are sure of the fit, the leading edges are tapered. The distinctive engine-cooling louvres are then stamped in, which is done with extreme care on four fly-presses, two of which are for the right hand and two for the left. There are twenty-four louvres along each top half and twelve along the side, and they are of different sizes top and side. A pencil line drawn down the centre of the bonnet-half guides the men as they feed the panel through the louvre presses. Once the first one has been

Exaggerating the curvature of a bonnet half by bending it over the beech pole; ear defenders or ear plugs are vital, such is the volume of noise in the workshop.

Punching out holes in the bonnet hinge so it can be joined to both halves.

Ensuring a bonnet has a good fit before stamping the louvres.

Drilling out fixture holes in the bonnet hinge.

Stamping out the twenty-four louvres in the top of a bonnet half.

stamped, it is a simple matter to space out the rest against a template. There is a lip on the scuttle front which supports the trailing edge of the bonnet, making it level with the swage panel which covers the top of the bulkhead. Two small pieces of aluminium tacked onto the scuttle rail act as temporary fillets to get the swage set at the right level.

Mounting point for the bonnet catch marked out.

Cars congregate at one end of the tin shop to be winged and cowled. This Plus 4 four-seater is almost ready for the paint shop.

Not surprisingly, it takes a whole day to make a bonnet. Bonnet catches made in the machine shop are tried, a pair to a side, and then removed for the time being. The two bonnet halves are placed in the back of the car, as they will be painted separately and fitted in the final assembly area.

SOLDERING

On the opposite side of the workshop are the three soldering bays with brazing hearths where the petrol tanks and 4/4 radiators are made. These have been put together by one man for the last twelve months or so, doing six at a time; Plus 4 and Plus 8 radiators are farmed out these days as they are just too time consuming to make. It is a rather nice touch that they bother with an in-house radiator at all, so laborious does the job seem. The soldering process is quite straightforward, and satisfying to do, once you have the knack. Basically, the joints are first filed to a good fit, then flux is applied

Preparing to solder up the brass slats for the stone guard, which will be sent away for chroming.

Soldering up the edges of a fuel tank.

Drilling the inner wheelarch on a two-seater for seatbelt mountings; this fixing is so secure that the whole car can be suspended from it.

Foreman Geoff Brewer checking the headlamp cowls for accuracy of roundness.

with a brush to allow the spelter or solder to flow easily into and around the joint as it is melted by blow-pipe flame or soldering iron. The solder then runs as a viscous fluid. Excess solder is wiped away using dilute sulphuric acid. The brass slats which make up the distinctive Morgan stone-guard or radiator grille are bent to shape by hand and laid out in an arc on their frame, then soldered up here in batches of twenty-five before being sent away for chroming. They will be the final component fitted to the car.

Foreman Geoff Brewer joined Morgan in 1955, and his hearing faculties appear not to be in the slightest bit damaged, despite his work environment. He is to be seen keeping an eye on progress generally, helping with a problem such as a difficult gearbox cover fitting or something of the sort. His speciality these days is aligning the headlamp cowls, which are set in the upper part of the front panel, just impinging on the long sweeping front wing. It is vital that the wings are square with the rest of the car and not sagging. While the pictures were being taken for this book, Geoff was masterminding the re-winging of MMC 11, and we marvelled at the dexterity of foreman and assistant; everything was cut and fitted by eye. This was a one-off, but in the normal course of things, when Geoff is happy with the bodywork, the car is pushed out of the sheet metal shop and back up the hill to the paint shop.

7 Paint Shop

You can have your Morgan painted virtually any colour you like, because there are 35,000 colours in ICI's 2K acrylic range to choose from. It will cost a little extra, but you will be doing paint shop foreman Derek Gardner a big favour as it will give him a break from regular Connaught green. In fact, there are five standard colours in the Morgan range, which at the moment consists of red, indigo blue, Connaught green, royal ivory or black. As one might expect of a British sports car with a competition pedigree, the most popular colour is the green, which closely matches the British Racing Green of Grand Prix machines before the advent of sponsor-bedecked liveries.

Psychology of colour choice is interesting. Red, well, red is the colour of the extrovert, as if the Morgan was not different enough in its own right, and I happen to think the standard Morgan red is a little on the pale side. Shades change from time to time, and I noticed some more appealing deeper rouges going through. A light, creamy colour like the royal ivory makes the contours of the body stand out, and has the advantage of being cooler under a blazing summer sun, whilst a black car is another kind of statement. In the late 1980s, so-called 'designer' fashion items had to be in black. I rate the indigo blue as the most subtle of the standard colours, although the dark Connaught green does unquestionably suit the car. I might personally be tempted to go for the sort of pale green which some ERAs and BRMs were painted. Everyone has their favourite of course, and I saw some striking choices whilst touring the factory. Two-tone mint green, like a Majorette model, two-tone

silver, or mustard yellow with a plain lacquered aluminium bonnet, for example. There were plenty of variations on the British Racing Green theme, sometimes darker like Morgan's former cellulose paint. Many have their wheels colour-coded, which if done in conjunction with the wing beading, looks most effective. There is an argument for having the car painted your favourite colour, however outlandish, since most people only have a brand-new Morgan once. But for the most part, customers stick to the regular colours. Derek Gardner will have checked the build ticket well in advance to make sure of the specified choice. He has been at Morgan for twenty years and has the impression that colour preferences come in waves. It used to be royal ivory, and after a run of green it may be a run of red. But at least he is thankful that there has been a trend towards diversification over the past ten years.

PAINTING PROCESS

In spite of the fact that the cars probably spend more time going through the painting process than any other department, the paint shop appears to be the least crowded of all the workshops, because there is no clutter of components lying around awaiting assembly; that is if you discount the bonnet halves and cowls which are stored here before final assembly. Also at least three cars will be hidden away in the painting booths. Before painting takes place, each car is fitted with an appropriate set of slave wheels, wires or alloys, with worn-out tyres,

Fresh from the tin shop, old wheels will be substituted, the wings unbolted, the interior and engine bay masked up.

which can get covered with paint. The tougher two-pack paint flexes with the bodywork rather than trying to remain like a shell and therefore cracking. At the same time as the switch to two-pack, the cars started to be painted with their wings off, which did away with the problem caused by paint cracking along the line where the

With wings removed the car is given an acid wash prior to filling.

123

New panels are treated to the acid wash to remove any impurities.

wings join the body. That area would from then on be properly protected. To allow the paint to get in, the front wings are detached slightly at the running board end, and the rears removed completely and put back on with a spacer between. The car is masked up, with the engine, dash area and spare wheel-well completely covered, but this is not the arduous job it once was, thanks to a system which supplies sheets of paper off a roll, ready taped. The roll of masking paper is mounted on a stand, made in the welding shop, and acts like a giant loo-roll holder. The person doing the spraying simply pulls off however much he needs and tears it off like kitchen paper. Masking up a car takes half an hour.

With wings akimbo front and rear, the car is taken to the de-oxydizing booth in the far right-hand corner for its acid wash and sprayed with an acidic agent, which removes all traces of dirt and grease, and any rust on the raw steel sections, and the acid is flushed off with water. It is then sanded all over to make a key for the filler, so that it sticks to the metal.

Rubbing down the areas of filler.

The clean metal does not stay that way for long, as now it is time to have any slight wrinkles and undulations in the wings filled, and where the filing of the weld has left abrasions. This is all part and parcel of car manufacture, which used to be done by lead loading; legend has it that a considerable proportion of the weight of a Mark II Jaguar is comprised of lead filler. Morgans used to have more filler around the headlight area than they do now, also prone to crack as the body flexed, but modern welding techniques have improved jointing quality. The main areas for filling are along the welds and joins, such as where the Morgan headlights join the wings. Although lead loading is still carried out, Morgans today rely on modern epoxy resin fillers, where a catalyst is mixed with the resin and the paste is smeared on to the dips and blemishes to make them smooth and level.

This takes four hours, and once it has gone off, it is moved into a car-sized area compartmentalized by long heavy plastic curtains draped from the ceiling, where it is sanded down with wet and dry sandpaper. To start with, a small power sander is used, but in general its use is restricted because there is a risk of cutting right through the metal. Rubbing down by hand permits greater control of materials.

After the smoothing off process, which leaves the cars silver and pale matt grey, they enter the closed-off McDonald primer booth to be undercoated. Gone are the days of polyester spray-fillers, and instead, etch-primer is used to build up a base layer and show up any defects which may need more filler. Each car receives five coats of cream-yellow matt primer, each accomplished in a quarter of an hour. The priming stage takes about three to three and a half hours, allowing for drying time, and then another four hours for two men to flat it off, dry, with orbital sanders and then wet, using 600-grade wet-and-dry paper.

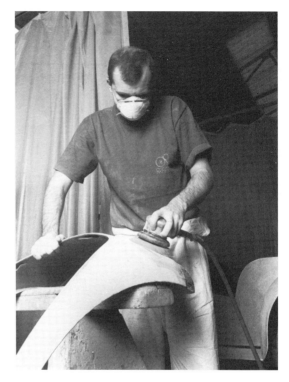

The cowl is steel, so a powder sander can be used.

The car is masked up again and wheeled into the booth at the opposite end of the department for its final coat and bake. The cowl and bonnet halves are laid out on a trestle with the car to be sprayed. A trial coat is applied and rubbed down, making sure there are no imperfections, then two finishing coats complete the job. Again, it is roughly fifteen minutes per coat, with a gap of several minutes between each one. A measure of the worth and durability of two-pack is that in the days of cellulose, a car would receive eight or nine coats of colour to build up the right depth and finish. The booth works by drawing hot air in from the top, directing it over the car and dispersing unwanted spray mist in the process, and ducted away via extractor vents in the sides of the chamber.

Every car gets five coats of matt primer, which takes roughly three hours including drying time.

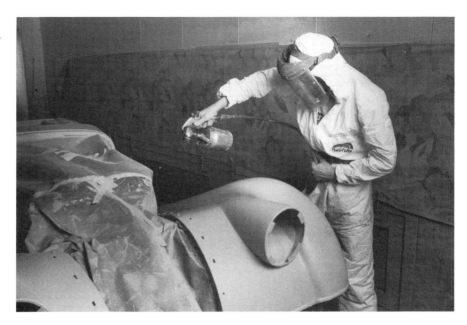

The transition from a cellulose finish, hand-painted with brushes in the thirties, to modern two-pack pigment was made in October 1986. The problem with cellulose was that it was brittle and subject to cracking, because Morgan bodies are given to flexing. This was responsible for numerous corrosion problems as the cracked paint flaked and let moisture in. Two-pack produces a better gloss than cellulose, although one

Getting the colour on; the first of two twin-pack top coats is applied.

advantage of the old method is that it can be used with few hazards at home in a DIY restoration.

Fully masked up himself, like some nuclear-age warrior, the sprayer then gets to work, spraying from a distance of about 18in (45cm). The gun is held between waist and chest height, and the sprayer's hand goes backwards and forwards triggering five-second bursts of coloured cloud, moving briskly and steadily, covering the undercoat and gradually working his way around the car. The finishing coat takes three and a half hours to achieve, including masking up, and the car then spends thirty-five minutes hardening off in the oven. It is then pushed out of the booth into the main workshop where it will be reunited with its proper wheels, bonnet and cowl. Coloured bonnet halves stand sentinel on a shelf which runs the length of the paint shop.

It takes four or five days for a car to go through the paint shop, and longer still if a lacquer coat is to be applied; everybody's workload averages out at two cars per day.

Restoration and repair work has to be accommodated as well, and they try hard to get it right first time since correcting blemishes involves a full mask-up and perhaps removing the wings again. The final result is a luxuriant high gloss, as thick and as smooth as it looks, and miles better than any production line paint job.

FITTING THE WING BEADING

The finished cars are then sent two by two across the factory road to the winging shop, a small room on the outer corner of the trim shop. There is only room for a pair at a time, and the task is to have the wing beading tacked on. All cars have wing beading now, and it ensures there is no possibility of corrosion between the cowl and alloy wings. Together with a coating of Waxoyl, it acts as a damp-proof course and a buffer between wing and body. There is a choice of colours: black, red or cream, and of course a contrasting

After painting, the car goes to have the wing beading fitted and the wings and cowl re-attached.

Once the wings are refitted, the wiring loom is installed, in this case in a Plus 4.

beading can set the body colour off nicely. The wings are bolted back on with four zinc-plated screw bolts, as is the cowl, but the bonnet does not get fitted until the end of the final assembly stage for ease of access to the engine bay.

Now the cars go back to the main block, to the wiring shop which is directly across the road in the entrance to the wood shop. The method was explained to me by 'Desperate' Dan Monk, a peripatetic employee of the repair shop who helps out in wiring when required. The looms are made up and supplied by David Bird of V-Lec in Bury, Lancs. They arrive in a bag, and are removed and rolled out flat. There is a right front and left

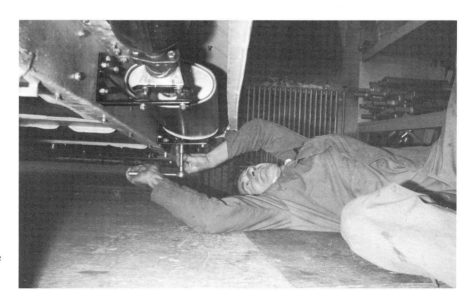

Fitting a Plus 4 exhaust; note the substantial brackets and secure mounting.

The Morgan F-series Super Sports three-wheeler, produced between 1933 and 1951, apart from a gap during the war, was powered by a four-cylinder 10hp Ford engine. In 1951 the F Super cost £333 including purchase tax.

This 4–4 four-seater drophead coupé of 1939 is typical in having full-height doors and no louvres in the top of the bonnet. Hub caps have been removed.

This 1964 4/4 four-seater is a Series V model fitted with the Ford Cortina's 1,498cc engine, and had a rear track two inches wider than previous 4/4s. The luggage rack is an essential extra for touring four-up.

The Plus 4 Plus was an attractive coupé made between 1964 and 1967, in fibreglass on a regular Plus 4 chassis and powered by the TR4/4A engine. Only 26 were built because despite the iconoclasm of the 'swinging sixties', customers preferred the traditional Morgan shape.

A Plus 4 Super Sports won the GT class at Le Mans in 1962, and this is the similar car of John Macdonald leading a Jaguar at Silverstone in 1973.

The widest Morgan ever made was John Macdonald's RUP 10M. Fitted with an Allard supercharger, this Plus 8 developed 550bhp and walked away with most races including this one at the 1974 Silverstone Bentley Driver's Club meeting.

The registration number MMC 11 appears here on a 1984 fuel-injected Plus 8 road test car. Being a factory plate, it has seen service on more than one Morgan, but principally Charles Morgan's ProdSports-winning car in 1978.

By 1986 when this Plus 8 was built, serious conservation measures had been instituted, including painting the chassis and dipping the wood frame in Cuprisol.

Purposeful-looking ProdSports racing Plus 8 of Graham Bryant is a 1988 car, with modified suspension, bumpers removed and roll-cage fitted.

The Plus 4 looks good in the factory colour indigo blue, with contrasting red wing beading and upholstery. This 1988 car is powered by the M16 Rover engine with 5-speed gearbox.

The Morgan factory has one of the most picturesque backdrops anywhere, being at the foot of the Malvern hills; here a Plus 8 is taken for an excursion.

London agent Bill Wykeham teamed up with Ludovic Lindsay to compete in the legendary Carrera Panamericana. Bill's 1956 Plus 4 finished first in class and fifth overall in 1990 and second in class and fourth overall in 1991.

The 4/4 featuring this exotic paint job is John Shealley's race car in America. He has been US National Sprint Champion Class C for the last five years.

The 4/4 two-seater continues to use the narrower body, its taller tyres providing tail-out handling. With more power available, the 1800cc Ford Zeta engine enhances these traditional Morgan characteristics.

The Plus 8 acquired telescopic dampers in 1991, attached to a rear cross tube and triangular plates on the chassis. This 1992 model is fitted with 6.5in alloy wheels and 205VR60 × 15 Pirelli P600 tyres.

Before the car goes to be trimmed, lights and indicators are fitted in the wiring and exhaust department.

front, and these bundles of wires are traced through the bulkhead and fixed to the panels. The rear loom is all of a piece, and logically this runs along the sides of the inner panels and round the back of the car. It is colour-coded, red and green on the left and green and white on the right. The relevant lights are then connected up to it. Rear lights are screwed in place here, and exhausts are fitted in the same bay; whilst this is a straightforward operation, it takes longer with the catalytic converters.

8 Trim and Final Assembly

The building that houses the trim, final assembly and finishing/testing departments was bought by Morgan in 1972, and work began there on 12 February 1973. Like the rest of the factory, it is a single-storey building but virtually all open plan, with the three departments merging imperceptibly with one another so that you are presented with a sea of Morgans, quite the largest array of cars in one place. They are all in varying stages of completion, and the largest number are in the throes of having trim fitted. It is almost impossible to say exactly what stage a particular car is at, because they go alternately from trim to final assembly and back again several times. An open plan department is an ideal arrangement because there is so much overlap in the build process at this stage. Things must have been pretty cramped in the original factory with the three extra shops housed there.

To make sense of the bewildering array of activities, a description of the layout of the department is in order. Internally, it is effectively a large 'L' shape, with an outside room where the cars get their wing beading fitted. Down one side of the department are benches where the trimmers shape, cut and make the pieces of upholstery which they will use to cover the casing panels. To the right are four lady machinists who sit at benches and sew up the hoods, tonneau and seat covers on what look like regular sewing machines, and they get everything sewn up to a point where it is ready for when a particular car needs it. Beside this area is the table where hoods, tonneau covers, all the carpets and gearbox covers are cut out. There are further benches down the far side of the building where seat upholstery takes place. The bottom of the L-shaped room is given over to the final assembly, finishing and testing sections.

LEATHER SELECTION

To one side is a caged-off area, in one corner of which are rolls of carpet and leather in different shades and black PVC material. Here is the 'office' of trim shop foreman Charlie Styles, who calculates how many hides to order of which colour, and allocates the specified materials to the cars in hand. Black PVC known as 'Ambla' is standard issue, but Connnolly hide in almost any stain is available at extra cost, and these days almost all customers ask for leather. There are seven standard shades, in addition to which a customer can specify virtually what he or she likes. The exotica comes from Connolly's 'Autolux' range, which has to be ordered specially, usually as soon as Charlie Styles receives the build ticket. This is particularly important as the wilder shades may take six weeks or more to arrive. Whilst leather is a more expensive option than Ambla PVC, the Autolux range is dearer still. It takes approximately four hides to upholster a two-seater, which absorbs an amazing 185 square feet of

Tools at the ready, the hoodmaker prepares to cut out his material.

leather. A four-seater uses four and a half hides, although one would imagine the extra seats would account for more than the extra half a hide. The largest hides are a little under 60 square feet, and the smallest around 34 square feet, and the best area is the animal's shoulders and back.

Most leather comes from Scandinavia at the moment, but it can be sourced from all over the world. There were some startling

Small sections of trim are marked out before cutting.

colours to be seen; a two-tone metallic green car was down for mint green leather, and a yellow four-seater Plus 4 was to have yellow leather upholstery, and I also saw garnet, an attractive maroon. Some customers are hard to please. One took delivery of his car, only to decide that he wanted green piping around the existing stone trim. This could only be achieved by unpicking all the stitching around the seats and the casings; in short, it would be a long job. He was advised it would work out cheaper to start again with a complete retrim, and that was what happened. The car ended up with magnolia leather and green piping. The customer paid of course.

There are so many possible shades that it would be impossible to maintain a stock of all but the most common hues. The seven standard colours are calculated to match or complement the five regular paint finishes. Almost predictably, they are black, red, blue, green, stone, light and dark brown. Some Autolux colours are very similar to the standard ones, but so particular are Morgan customers that of the thirty or so cars present on one of my visits, only three were trimmed in standard colour leather. That said, colours tend to come in runs for some reason, so that for some weeks they get to do all the drab stone and browns, and suddenly there is a run of bright colours. There can be no rational explanation for this; purely chance.

If leather has been ordered, all panels will be upholstered in that medium; there is no combination of leather and PVC. The volume of cars clad in leather is now 95 per cent. That is to say perhaps one car a month is done in PVC, which is a change even from a decade or so ago. Twenty years ago it was very rare to have one trimmed in leather. But leather has a sexier tactile quality about it than synthetic PVC, and with Connolly's special treatment, it is also more durable for an open-top sports car. From a manufacturing point of view though, vinyl is easier to work than leather, but not as nice to work with.

In addition to trimming the cars in-build, the trim shop, like all other departments, also has to provide its share of hoods, tonneau covers and sundry trim sections for restoration jobs. There will be at least one complete retrim for an older car in the workshop at any given time. The oldest retrim as far as Charlie Styles is concerned has been a 1952 car, and he has been with the company since 1956. He can supply sections going back forty years, and he says they should fit; if not, then the car must have been altered, which of course is possible in that space of time. The longevity of an interior depends much on how the car is looked after, and clearly, if it is constantly exposed to the elements it will not last more than six or seven years. Charlie Styles recommends using mild soap followed by Connolly's hide food when cleaning leather every two or three months; it will keep it supple and increase the life span enormously. Charlie is a model Morgan employee. He came straight from school aged 15, and completed a six-year apprenticeship. For the next six months he was categorized as semi-skilled, before going on to the top rating. He became foreman in 1965, which makes him the longest serving foreman, although other foremen have been with the company slightly longer. The cars are still being trimmed today just as they were when he joined in 1956.

Thirteen people are employed on the upholstery side. One is called the labourer who does the fetching and carrying and sweeping up. Everything to go on the car is laid out on it in neat piles. Although everything is numbered, some shades of leather may be visually close; thus maroon 893 is very similar to maroon 3,185, and it is essential to get it right at the outset. If it was just laid out on the bench, the materials could be

Pattern template for the door panel.

Using a template, leather is cut for an interior panel.

Tacking trim in place after cutting out.

Cutting out the lining for the back of a seat.

Gluing up the rubber crash padding on the scuttle ready for its trim.

inadvertently muddled up. The process gets under way when three trimmers make up the casings, the backing boards which form the car's inner panels, then they take the specified material and cut out the shapes against the appropriate templates. Once the

cutting out has taken place, the trimmer is committed. He will have checked the leather for holes and marks, caused by barbed wire, or in the case of hides from Africa, warple fly, whose grubs burrow out from under the beast's skin. Most imperfections occur in the

Trimming the rubber crash padding above the dashboard.

area of the beast's belly, and many will stretch out. Other blemishes are hidden in a tuck or the hide discarded altogether if they are too bad. But for the most part, the hides are very good quality. Preparation takes about two hours, and then each of the men starts to attach the sections to the car he is working on. The material has been glued or pinned onto the panels. The door capping has the leather tacked on first; then there is an elbow iron which goes inside, and a roll of sorbo rubber sits on top, and the leather is rolled neatly over and pinned on the side. They work swiftly and confidently, a practised eye telling them exactly where each tack or screw has to go, where each tuck and fold belongs, and the operation takes four hours. The first step is to cover the wheelarches, then the rockers, swage panel and the armrests. While that is being done, the casing boards are being covered. The crash padding around the top of the dashboard or scuttle rim is made of one piece of rubber now (formerly two) and it is covered with the trim material.

Naturally there is more work involved trimming a four-seater because the wheelarches are more in evidence, and these have to be trimmed to start with; there are different casing boards, and of course there are the rear seats themselves to take care of. The Plus 4 four-seater with its wider Plus 8 body and wings has an extra two inches in the back between the wheelarches, and as we saw in the wood shop, the back end of the four-seaters has been wider since the 1992 Motor Fair. The size differences between the two models are more obvious in the bulkier four-seater cars, and even more evident in the now-discontinued 4/4 four-seater, which was a couple of inches taller still and had a much more traditional look about it. The differences are in the height of the bulkhead, the windscreen, and the doors and side panels are correspondingly taller. The four-seater Plus 4 is two inches higher than its two-seater counterpart at 52in (132cm). This compares with the Plus 8, which is a low-slung 48in (122cm).

Fastenings are inserted in the scuttle crash padding, whilst the hood-frame webbing is attached to the tonneau deck; inner panels have already been trimmed.

Fixing the padding in place that covers the top of the door.

DIFFERING HOODS

The four-seater hood is a lot more complicated than the two-seater's, with its extra material, perspex windows and turnbuttons.

It is obviously a longer job. Then there is a separate hood frame cover which fits over the folded-down hood behind the rear seats. There are four separate sidescreens with sliding windows, and the four-seater also

A four-seater hood frame is installed; unlike the two-seater hood frame, it is made by an outside supplier, and will be powder-coated once the hood has been made up.

137

Hoods

The hood is one item of equipment that most Morgan owners are happy to do without, preferring to enjoy the elements and simply cover the cockpit with a tonneau when stationary. Hoods have always been supplied though, ranging from the relatively sophisticated three-position foldaway example of the Series I coupé to its lift-off counterpart on the two-seater. There was no attempt at rear threequarter windows, with just a crinkly celluloid rectangle at the back. Hood material was a close-weave cotton known as duck, and it was stretched over a frame which folded behind the seats, and attached around the rim with lift-a-dot fasteners and turnbuckles.

Sidescreens are steel-framed, originally covered in the same material as the hood with celluloid windows which quickly yellowed to opaqueness. Now they are much sturdier with a PVC covering and sliding perspex windows. By the time the Plus 4 was launched in 1950 there was an opening flap at the base through which hand signals were made. Fixing details for sidescreens changed with virtually every model. Coupés had a small circular-ended glass window, whilst the four-seater with its pram-like shape, which allowed greater headroom in the back, was given rear threequarter windows and additional windows in the sidescreens. A half-tonneau was standard issue, a full tonneau optional.

From the early 1960s, sliding window sidescreens were optional on a Plus 4 making the signals flap redundant. The two-seater hood was now made with rear threequarter windows, although the 4/4 hood continued to have just the rear window. In all cases, the hood irons were joined together by tapes so that the hoops were equidistant. By 1969, the four-seater was endowed with much larger rear threequarter windows and sliding sidescreen windows; there was a second set for the rear seat passengers. The hood is still separate from the frame today, although a full tonneau became standard two-seater equipment from 1975, whilst the four-seater has a hood cover.

Fibreglass hard tops are made by Rutherford Engineering, and provide the Morgan owner with snug winter transport; works competition car MMC 11 was equipped with a Rutherford hard top.

Sidescreens are made in PVC by an outside supplier and fitted in final finish.

has a larger tonneau cover. Four-seater hood frames are made outside by a specialist, unlike the two-seater's, and they do not get powder-coated until the hood has been fitted and Charlie Styles is happy everything folds up and down properly. Before the car goes off to dispatch, the hood is removed and the bare metal frame taken off for powder-coating. The reason for this is that they are made by hand, and having such a specialized

Assisted by clamps and wooden supports, a windscreen is fitted in final finish.

collapsible mechanism, it makes sense to make sure everything fits before painting in case anything has to be altered. Two-seater hood frames are apparently virtually foolproof and are powder-coated as soon as they leave the machine shop where they are made.

At this stage the cars go to final assembly to get their windscreens put on. They also fit the sidescreens and hood frames, followed by gearbox and prop-shaft covers. Then the car returns to the trimmers who install the upholstered casing panels on the doors, and the floor areas are carpeted. Choice of colour for the carpet is normally left to the trim shop, and they will match the standard carpets as closely as possible to the shade of the rest of the upholstery and car colour, unless otherwise instructed. Some customers want their wheelarches or rocker panels trimmed in carpet, and most special requests and mix and match can be fitted in. Some areas are padded, like the rockers, and the padding is felt and jiffy-foam, a water-repellent material which coats the felt and makes it impervious to rain water. To the untutored eye, the most difficult piece of trim is the band of piping which runs from the door, back round the elbow and around the back of the car. This is made up of a piece of leather which is glued up and folded over around a piping cord, and sewn down by a machinist. It is then pinned all the way around the car. To achieve this, a screwdriver is inserted under the piping by the trimmer, twisted to expose the frame, the pin is tacked in, and the piping goes back over the frame. It is called 'hidem banding', and the pins are invisible from the outside.

The hood and tonneau are also under way now, and they will be ready for fitting when the car is fully equipped. The standard hood is made of PVC, but an optional extra is the mohair hood, and if this is specified, the sidescreens are covered to match; they come in from the supplier, Groves of Wolverhampton,

in PVC. Standard hoods are unlined, and come in black as standard, but there are seven possible colour choices in the Everflex range. The mohair hoods are properly known as German Rivenhoods, and are similar to those seen on the leading Teutonic cabriolets. They are fitted to about a third of Morgan production now. They are thicker, more durable, and feel more like canvas, and there is no doubt they look and feel better than the regular PVC hoods. They enhance the appearance of a car, and that kind of quality does not come cheap; to equip your four-seater thus with hood, tonneau and hood cover will cost almost an extra £1,000. It even sews up better than the standard material, although the needles have to be changed more often. The perspex for the rear window is bought in and cut to fit, and the machinists sew it in. At this point in the procedure the hood is half sewn up, and then it is stretched over the hood frame, and marked off around the screen. Each hood and tonneau cover is sewn up individually and tailored exactly to each car. There is no question of simply taking one out of stock as it would probably not fit.

The gearbox covers and the transmission tunnel are covered over next; the material is simply glued on to the shaft cover, and machined up with felt behind and buttoned onto the floor by the gearbox cover, in case access is needed to the mechanicals. Among the last trimming jobs are the gaiters for gear lever and handbrake, and the door retaining straps. Sometimes speakers have to be accommodated; whether or not one wants to install a radio or tape player, there is some sense in having speakers fitted at this stage as it is always something of an upheaval getting them slotted in at a later date. Meanwhile two men cut the seat fabric out and prepare the stuffing, using a hard foam, and taking a couple of hours per seat. There are eighteen pieces of material to each bucket seat, and every one is tailored

Sections of a hood are machined up; standard hoods are unlined, with a choice of seven colours in the Everflex range.

individually. The lady machinists sew up the panels into covers. Having done the seats, the trimmer starts on the door trims for the next car. While the seats are being made

ready the car goes back across the department to final assembly for its facia board to be fitted, into which goes the dash panel. One man is responsible for the dashboard

Four lady machinists are responsible for sewing up the hoods and their perspex windows, the tonneau covers, seat covers and carpets.

Wiring up the instrument panel before the dashboard is fitted.

and its fittings; it may be clad in leather, or for an extra cost, traditional walnut veneer. Apart from the dials, warning lights and switches, it may include extra map light, clock and radio. The seats will be ready for fixing in the car when it is ready to go to the finishing area.

Other final assembly functions include

Front passenger seat is installed in a left-hand drive four-seater.

A length of stainless steel strip is added to the threshold of the door aperture.

the fitting of seatbelts, front and rear if applicable, which is done once the casings are trimmed; twenty turnbuttons for the hood fixings, and filler caps (the 4/4's was on the left until 1991 when it was moved to the right under a locking panel; the Plus 4's is also on the right, and the Plus 8 of course has a filler on both sides). The torpedo side-lights on the wing tops are unique. They are made by LAP, sub-contracted from Lucas.

Everything is tested to make sure it is working, such as the lights and electrical components. The hoses are checked for leaks and the brakes are tested. Don Passey is foreman of the finishing shop. He joined Morgan in 1952 and started off in the repair shop, moving to the chassis assembly shop until 1971. He then took over the Chief Tester Charlie Curtis's job when final assembly was back where the chassis shop is today. There was far more pushing the cars up and down in those days, recalls Don; the reorganization came with the acquisition of the present trim/final assembly/finishing shop. When a car reaches finishing stage, it must all come together.

The final act is to underseal the cars, assuming the customer has asked for it. This is done in a neighbouring workshop by an outside contractor. The cars are completed at a rate of two a day by just one person, each taking two hours to do. They are hoisted up on a ramp with wheels removed, and all hidden inner sections are sprayed with Waxoyl; then the undersides of the floor, wheelarches and spare wheel well are liberally undersealed in a thorough operation.

TESTING TIME

Testing of the cars is carried out by Tony Monk, who since 1976 has been the first person to give each one its baptism on the road. His first act is to fit the steering wheel which he torques up with a wrench. Then the car is given a run to warm it up, and it is brought back to have its ignition timing checked and the exhaust emissions calibrated on a CO meter. Steering, brakes and exhaust mountings are checked for

Final stop on the build process is the Waxoyl and undersealing bay; each car spends two hours here.

tightness, and the car then gets a second outing of about twenty miles. A final check, and it is handed over to the dispatch shop.

Lined up awaiting delivery on either side of the dispatch shop are two rows of pristine Morgans. The final touches are added here: front bumpers and stone guards, and a final polishing. There is invariably a tiny bit of sprucing up to do to one car or another, a bit of trimming to finish off or an under-bonnet touch-up. There was a problem with birds nesting in this department, with the

A Plus 4 on its maiden voyage, leaving final finish for its first venture into the outside world.

As Chief Tester, Tony Monk has the privilege of being the first person to drive every car; he gives each car two outings, the second of which covers about twenty miles.

The stone guard and bumpers are fitted when the car gets to the dispatch bay.

attendant nuisance of acidic birdlime dropping on the cars' brand-new paintwork; everyone has had to cope with paint finishes despoiled in this way, and unless you wash it off promptly, it etches its way into the paint surface. On freshly painted cars, sitting with their tops down, it must have been particularly galling. The problem was finally cured by the introduction of a stuffed owl, which acted as a deterrent to the smaller birds nesting there.

9 Repair Shop

The repair shop is at the top end of the factory, tacked on behind the dispatch bay. As the name implies, they do repair work, but also servicing and restorations, and race preparation. The assembled Morgans I saw were probably typical of the department's regular workload. Amongst a handful of modified Morgans in varying stages of race-readiness was a car wearing Libra Motive logos, which has been campaigned of late by Rob Wells; foreman Mark Baldwin explained that good old MMC 11 was awaiting restoration to its former appearance as Charles's late seventies mount in order to take part in the Morgan race series in 1993. A more standard-looking car was the 'works' car, which the factory enters for Charles in classic events like the Tour de France. This was BUY 600M, a car with many successes to its credit. A red car was identified as Bruce Stapleton's contender for the 1993 re-run of the London–Sydney Marathon, although now it is bright yellow with outrageous 'kangaroo bars' at the front. The repair shop was getting preparation up to a certain stage before Stapleton took over. Otherwise, there is the occasional warranty job, and more significantly, the repair shop puts into action the fruits of Bill Beck's endeavours in development.

Nearly all the remaining cars were restoration projects, going back to a 1955 flat-rad Plus 4, which came in two years ago and might be ready in another six months. This had a TR3 engine, and its steering column had just been replaced. The Smiths gauges and switches would be difficult to replace, and it was unlikely that the car would finish up with much of its original equipment on it.

Several of the cars do not amount to more than a pile of bits or else are empty shells, because they have been stripped right down and await whatever new tackle is needed to refettle them. This may have to come from any of the other departments. If a restoration is a chassis-up rebuild, the car will progress through the factory along with the normal production cycle. It may return to the repair shop between each stage to have some work done before going off to the next major hurdle. Usually any metalwork is done specially by Geoff Brewer, but if only a wing or two is required, the repair shop will get the necessary item from stores and fit it themselves. If wings and cowl are wanted, the car will almost certainly have a new bonnet made as the old one will not fit the other new panels. So Mark has to be especially careful when estimating for a crash job, in order to take this possibility into account. The assessor will probably comment that nothing appears to be wrong with the bonnet, at which Mark will explain the nature of Morgan manufacture to him.

RESTORATIONS

Most customers understand how their car is made, but it is never completely clear what will be needed to do a restoration until the repair shop has stripped the car down to the bare essentials. Only then can the customer be given an accurate estimate. A factory restoration is a slow job, because the car has to be slotted in alongside other jobs and regular production. Consequently there is almost as long a waiting list for restorations

Carrying out a service in the repair shop; evidently one spotlight has a poor earth. Other cars are in for maintenance and restoration, and because it deals with every aspect of Morgan servicing, this department probably knows the cars as a whole better than any other.

as there is for a new car. The cost is not far behind either. There is a minimum price limit of £6–£7000, beneath which it just is not worth the factory's while to get involved. The ceiling for a complete rebuild is understandably going to be more or less the same as a new car, depending on what is usable from the wreck; with all new materials, why should it be any less? With the older cars, just dismantling can be difficult, although Morgan assembly does generally aid this process. A figure of £18,000 might cover a chassis-up job minus running gear. I was shown a one-year-old car which had been left in a garage where it had collected dust. Someone had wiped it clean and scratched it badly in the process, and now it was back to have a total respray. The special circumstances merited this car jumping the queue.

There is a policy that any car taken in will not be left outside, but occasionally it proves difficult to get hold of the owner when the job is done. Before long, he will be charged a parking fee because of the shortage of space.

There are concours enthusiasts and people who stick their cars on pedestals, and works manager Mark Aston is not entirely in accord with this view, seeing a car as something to be driven and enjoyed for itself; which is why he is running the Morgan Challenge racing championship. He has little sympathy for owners who come back to have minor problems sorted out which are down to the car only having done 1,000 miles (1,600km) in twelve months. Generally the 60,000 mile-a-year (96,000km) cars work out better than the cosseted part-timers. But as a rule not many cars made

One of the works' competition Plus 8s, BUY 600M, is in the repair shop for refettling and tuning. The car was driven to third place in its class in the 1992 Tour de France by Charles Morgan, with his wife Jane navigating.

after the Cuprisol treatment was instituted in 1986 are returned. According to Mark Baldwin, the anti-corrosion measures introduced over the last seven or eight years have totally transformed the longevity of the car. Mark is not even convinced of the need to galvanize the chassis, such is the strength of powder-coating; regular Waxoyling will suffice, he says. As to its survival, again, much depends on how the car is used. If it is a summer-only car and the winter storage is wrong for reasons of humidity, it will suffer more than a car used all year round, which has a chance to have the wind dry it out.

One reason why the repair shop is at the forefront of Morgan evolution is that it deals with the product after it has been out in the big wide world. Mechanical mayhem, crash carnage or corrosion crisis, they see it at its worst. Mark Baldwin has been at the factory for ten years, and he told me that Morgans stand up to accident damage very well. As testimony he recalled an accident in which the chassis had been deformed by a 100mph (160km/h) side impact so as to bend it like a banana, although it was still possible to sit in the cockpit. The cars seem to endure frontal impacts too. A Plus 8 owner apparently survived a 90mph (145km/h) impact with just a bruised rib. But these gory details don't inform or reassure us much. Morgan owners generally like to live life to the full, and if you really wanted to play safe, you would probably buy a Mercedes.

Beside one of the department's two hoists was Charles Morgan's 'blue car', the Plus 8 with the honeycomb chassis, no louvres in the bonnet and no sidelights on the wings. It is the nearest you will get to a unit-construction or monocoque Morgan. The whole underside of the car is a tub of aluminium honeycomb. It weighs 1,848lb (840kg), as opposed to the 2,068lb (940kg) dry weight of the standard car. It is the prototype for a number of new ideas; the lack of louvres in the bonnet is to test engine cooling. There are no bumpers, the suspension is not standard, and it sports BBS split-rim alloy wheels. The new type of wrap-around bucket seats are fitted in the bare untrimmed cockpit. They are good-looking seats, and you sit back into them rather than on top of the squab. The prototype of this radical chassis cost £750 from Ciba-Geigy, against more like £300 for a standard one.

A staff of four operates the repair shop, and they were at pains to disassociate themselves from other departments, which they say are not as much fun! Perhaps their relative youth has something to do with it, or their detachment from the actual build process which breeds a sort of independence. Because of the close liaison between repair shop and development, Bill Beck is a regular visitor. It was his province before Mark Baldwin took over, and in fact he originally interviewed Mark, whose father worked at the factory. For some reason Mark was the only applicant for the job, and without any preliminaries to speak of, was more or less asked when he could start. Mark took over as foreman in 1990, and clearly there is a good enthusiastic atmosphere in the department. The most exciting time is when Morgan club events are being staged, and it is impossible to move because of the streams of Morgans coming in to have small jobs done. Last year Mark was so rapidly overwhelmed that he had to abandon the job cards. In the end they just helped the drivers out with whatever problem they had in order to move the queue.

10 Development Shop

The man who shoehorned the first Buick engine into a Morgan and thus produced a quantum leap in the company's history was Maurice Owen, former development engineer. He is now part-time for a couple of days a week, and at the time of writing was the manager of the steering wheel boss air-bag project. He has put the cars through many of the tests for type approval legislation during the late 1980s and early 1990s. Now Maurice is semi-retired, and over the last couple of years, development has been handled by Bill Beck.

Previously Bill was foreman of the repair shop, the only department where they know the car inside out; in the 'tin shop' they are metallurgists, in trim it's the leather, but repair shop work encompasses the whole car, which means they have to be conversant with the entire vehicle rather than one particular aspect of it. There is no doubt that Bill has wrought many small changes which have improved and simplified the cars a great deal. His route to simplification is standardizing components where possible, and small things like engine mounting rubbers all add up. For instance, he has utilized the same engine-mounting brackets for the Plus 4 as for the 4/4's Zeta unit, although their placement on the chassis would be different. His task is to identify ways of improving the cars, hence his close liaison with the repair shop. Having thought of the idea, he then talks it through with the foreman of whichever shop would incorporate the modification to see if it would work in practice.

From the outside, the development shop is no more than an unassuming brick shed next door to the wood store. But once inside, there is no question of the seriousness of intent. My eyes alighted on a T16 engine fitted with a turbocharger. What was the meaning of this, I wondered. Earlier on when I ventured to ask Charles if the T16 turbo engine would be used in production Plus 4s, he said not, seeing the supercharger as a more appropriate means of forced induction for the Morgan. Yet here it was, a turbo T16 unit about to go into the development Plus 4 I had just been driving. I imagine the turbo to be the logical way of widening the gap between the Plus 4 and 4/4. The groundwork has already been done by Rover, and it could simply be offered as an option for speed-freaks. It will almost certainly come into the reckoning if used in the Morgan Challenge race series, being eligible from 1993.

Bill Beck had a more down to earth explanation. 'It's to do with tax breaks', he said. The Rover T16 turbocharged unit, known as the Tomcat, delivers 200bhp, which takes it into Plus 8 territory. But there is a considerable tax advantage in certain countries to running a car under 2.0-litres, which gives a Tomcat-engined Plus 4 a big advantage and makes it worth marketing in those countries. It would probably cost as much to make as a Plus 8, so there would be little difference in price between the two. Bill thought it unlikely that it would be labelled as a turbo; more likely a Plus 4 Tomcat. It can be boosted to 260bhp, but whether the Rover 200 transmission will take it is another question.

The Plus 8 gearbox is a different matter, however, and Bill was in the process of modifying a Plus 8 chassis, lowering its

Development chassis fitted with turbocharged T16-Tomcat engine. Exhaust pipe has been redesigned to avoid a left-hand drive pedal box.

Rear gearbox mounting point is now below rather than above chassis, straightening out the drive-train and lowering the centre of gravity; Plus 8 will reap other benefits.

gearbox rear mounting brackets from the top to the bottom of the chassis so that the engine would sit an inch-and-threequarters lower at the back, and the prop-shaft would be more in-line than at present. He intended to try a Plus 8 engine to make sure that it fitted, and then he would have it built up with a Tomcat engine as a complete running Plus 4. A new exhaust manifold had to be concocted because the standard T16 turbo unit would foul the brake master cylinder and pedal box in a left-hand drive car. Bill has also swapped over the battery location from the left to the right side of the car to improve weight distribution. A small gesture perhaps, but at the moment a Plus 4 has its exhaust on the left, and in a left-hooker, there is the driver's weight on that side too. So it is a matter of equalizing the ancilliaries. Other modifications would be built into the chassis for evaluation. Everything he wants to try goes on one car, and if it works, it is left on.

If a turbocharger takes the Plus 4 closer to the current Plus 8, it also has the effect of distancing it from the 1800cc 4/4, which develops 125bhp. Morgan's trump card would be to go to 4.5-litres with the Plus 8, and ignore the 4.2-litre unit in the process. Bill will have to spend some time on the axle in order for it to handle the extra power; this may well involve the fitting of anti-tramp bars. Doubtless he will find a way of doing it. He has pondered the virtues of going completely independent with the back suspension, but this would involve a fundamental redesign of the chassis. Adequate as it is at the moment, it would be flexing all over the place without the degree of stiffness offered by the solid rear axle and leaf spring arrangement; curiously enough these are rather like trailing arms as they come a relatively long way forwards. Bill Beck points out the merits of leaf springs from a maintenance point of view; they will still be good after 100,000 miles, whereas at 40,000,

an independent set-up will have wear in the lugs and start twitching in corners and need overhauling. He is looking at the front suspension as well, trying different dampers and seeing if the cars can do without the damper blade.

Bill jokes that the development shop is like his own Meccano set. It is certainly cramped in there; there is scarcely room to swing the proverbial tomcat. The other chassis in his hideaway was fitted with frame and sheet metal, but no running gear, and included the 3in longer doors intended for production. These contained the rectangular section aluminium tubes which withstand a side impact. The current four-seater doors are shorter than those of the two-seater, and it is intended that the four-seater will get the longer doors. One side effect of this is that Bill is having to redesign the hood frame, which will pivot from further back. He motioned me to the far side of the chassis-bodyshell. It had obviously been subjected to a side impact test. The metal was bowed and so was the wood, but he said that once the metal was removed, the wood would spring back to regain its original shape and would be used again. That was after a pressure of two tons had been exerted. The door lock gave way 330lb (150 kilos) short of the two tons, so there will have to be a door jamb fitted.

AIRBAG

He was also working on the airbag system, experimenting with other manufacturers' solutions to the problem. Because the Morgan has a flat steering wheel, there is a need to get more distance between the wheel and the crash padding so knuckles are less vulnerable. The airbag provides the answer as it is installed in a dished steering wheel, which provides that distance, but as a consequence the driving seat will have to be

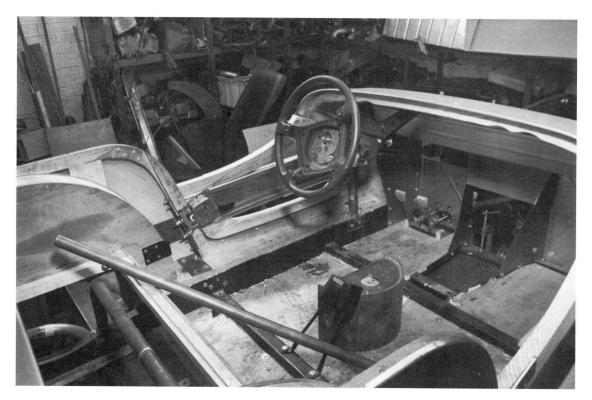

Work in progress on a mule chassis for Californian legislation; fillets strengthen the scuttle, pedals have been brought back by 1.5in, steering wheel 3in to improve clearance between wheel and dashboard. As a consequence, the driving seat will move back too.

Door is some three inches longer for ease of access, and incorporates aluminium side-impact beam.

moved back some 3in (7.5cm), and the pedals by 1.5in (3.75cm). 'This is a bit of a pain really,' said Bill, clearly understating the matter. Mercifully, these modifications will apply only to cars destined for California for the time being. A man with a very practical mind, he was also considering how to alter the frame to allow for storage space behind the seats, which is radical stuff for enthusiasts who like touring but hate luggage racks. He was talking about two suitcases going sideways behind the seats, and thought this could be achieved by moving the heel board right back as though it was a four-seater. The battery would be relocated; the toolbox which has always lived on the metal front will be moved, and its future location is still at the discussion stage.

In the course of getting the airbag properly installed, he is modifying the scuttle panel, or metal front as he calls it, because there is insufficient strength at the centre to withstand a detonation of the airbag. He has inserted fillets to strengthen it, which he believes also means it is easier to make. With this alteration to the scuttle panel, the gearbox cover will be a much smaller affair, and the inside of the car is 'tidied up a bit'. Its first try-out will be in the Plus 4 with the Tomcat engine, and if it works, he will take it a stage further and install the airbag steering wheel. 'Best not to do too much all at once,' he says. Another benefit which will come with lowering the gearbox mountings on the Plus 8 chassis is that the entire drive train will be lowered, so that it will no longer be necessary to remove the water pump before the engine is installed. It can stay where it is, and the bonnet will close over it. It may also be possible to leave the clutch housing in its extended position instead of transferring the master cylinder to the top of the bellhousing. The lower transmission height affects the position of the gear lever of course, so there would be effectively more room between gearbox

cover and dashboard. Gear levers will in future be straight rather than crooked, which will make reverse gear much easier to engage. Such practical thinking stems from Bill's background in garages, trucks and earth-moving vehicles, chain-saws, and caravans. During his time in the repair shop he dealt directly with cars in everyday use and was often thinking to himself, 'I'll change that!' or 'I'd like to get hold of the idiot who designed that!' 'Now,' he said, 'I am in just that position, so I have to come up with the right answers.' He believes that there are too many alternatives and anomalies, and he would like to see as many components standardized as is helpful for production. There is no doubt that these improvements will be beneficial, and, he continues, 'It will be much easier to make them work because I discuss them with the chaps who make the cars. Keep them involved so they know what's in the pipeline.'

AERODYNAMICS

Bill Beck is critical of the Plus 8's burgeoning front end; it is getting out of proportion, he thinks. But it is not the shape of the front end so much as the flat windscreen which limits the Morgan's aerodynamics. Competition-style aeroscreens help reduce the frontal area; the trouble is that an open car has a worse drag coefficient than a closed coupé. Wind tunnel tests carried out at MIRA six years ago and by the German *Auto Motor und Sport* magazine pegged the cd figure of a closed Plus 8 at 0.42. The cut-aways around the headlights are beneficial to air-flow, and the car is stable in side-winds. Purely by chance, it was noted that there is considerable downforce above the wheels. Less helpful are the sidelights and louvres. One obvious move would be to incorporate the sidelights into the

The battery has swapped sides to equalize weight distribution and counter the exhaust system in a four-cylinder car. The fuel tank will be redesigned to accommodate the new spare wheel housing.

headlights, but the louvres are both cosmetically and practically desirable. The tests showed that there are small areas of wind resistance just ahead of the rear wings as well. The Morgan's flat plywood floor is a contributor to its slippery shape, because there are few protrusions beneath the car.

Apart from the airbag, Bill is also responsible for incorporating other items deemed necessary by legislation. 'The most difficult thing is keeping the cars looking like real Morgans,' he said. This is because some legislation is more difficult for a Morgan to incorporate than it is for a more conventional car. It is not just catalysts and so on now; as well as dealing with the driving position (which may produce a better ride, ironically, as you are nearer still to the back axle where the ride comes from) he is lowering the spare wheel deeper into the rear panel. This is partly cosmetic, because as the wheels have got wider, so the spare has gained more and more prominence to the point of looking a trifle absurd. The plan is to have just 1.5in (3.75cm) of spare standing proud of the rear

panel. More seriously, we may soon see the introduction of new brake light legislation which calls for a centre-mounted brake light. Rather than mount the light up some incongruous stalk so that it sits in the middle of the rear window like a Volvo estate, by depressing the wheel further into the rear panel and shifting the spare wheel well downwards, it should be possible to mount the hypothetical new brake light on a small plinth in the space above the spare. But it does not end there. It means redesigning the fuel tank, and Bill has already drawn a new one, which will be squarer, but with a 45 degree angle behind the spare wheel. It will probably be larger than existing tanks with a capacity of 16.5 gallons (74l) instead of the Plus 8's present 12 gallons (54l).

So the development shop is a hive of activity; much of it emanating from Bill Beck's fertile brain and his application of practical knowledge. By going over his schemes with the workforce, the cars will continue to incorporate the very latest technology without changing the way they are made.

11 Legislation

The onerous task of legislation analysis falls on Works Manager and Assistant Managing Director Mark Aston. This is definitely the 'short straw'. A technical designer, he has worked his way up through the factory since 1976, and from 1982 his wide-ranging brief was to oversee the activities of the repair shop, to be involved with production and development and general hiring and firing, taking into account wages, health and safety and other changes in the factory.

Mark looks after legislation-imposed changes on the cars; also employees' training, which generates mountains of paperwork and has to be rigorously adhered to; and legislation in the factory itself. One example is the Environmental Protection Act, which deals with emissions from factories, and which Morgan is obliged to register for, listing all the processes undertaken. Legislation seems incredibly boring, but the bureaucrats have the power to stop Morgan or anybody else making cars instantly; one breach of the regulations and that is that. The company could be ruined by the casual stroke of a clerk's pen. Although at times Morgan may feel itself to be first in line as the environmental lobby's whipping boy, actually they do not often look at Morgans; it is more often the pap of the major manufacturers that comes under scrutiny, and those in the ivory towers invent new rules such as bumpers and frontal surfaces having to be made of pedestrian-friendly deformable plastic. This might help if you are clobbered at 5mph, but will not make a lot of difference at 30 or 40mph. But it means Morgan cannot change their front bumper until they know precisely what the new legislation will be. There is another nefarious proposal which talks about a maximum angle of 45 degrees between the front line of the car, which is from the edge of the bumper, to the top of the cowl. The implication of this would be to project the bumper forwards and in some way lower the cowl. How this could be done with an in-line engine is a mystery.

Depressingly, Mark sees only increasing bureaucracy and more and more paperwork, and it struck me how opposite all that is to the freedoms afforded by the cars themselves. A little of it is justified, like factory emissions, but Mark reckons 'An awful lot of it looks like a method of maintaining employment for bureaucrats, particularly in Brussels.' The SMMT in London is very helpful in providing lists of relevant legislation within the motor industry each month, and Mark pulls out perhaps seventy items a month which are relevant to Morgan which he has to take home and read. Rover employs 250 people to handle legislation, mostly qualified lawyers. Mark hopes it will not be long before Morgan employs one too. Much of the proposed legislation is at draft stage, so there is still time to argue against it. These days it takes only six months for it to be ratified. When protrusions and projections were on the agenda, prospects looked bleak for Morgan, but the major manufacturers protested too, concerned they would have to scrap existing tooling, and threatened to shut up shop and go elsewhere. The ensuing legislation was responsible for the current spate of rounded jelly moulds with recessed door-handles, but with no new car to launch, Morgan could breathe again.

157

Enjoying a Morgan seems light years away from the mounting bureaucracy which has to be negotiated in order to produce the cars.

Mark admits there is a tendency to become conservative about Morgan, but thinks that change for the sake of it is a mistake. Change is not a bad thing as long as there is a good reason for it, such as the Morgan's rear dampers. Mark is cynical about certain new developments. One is safety, which is used to sell cars now. Undersized side-impact bars which have not been tested are marketing tools and often not a lot of good in practice. There is no European standard for airbags, and the German bag is much smaller than the Californian one, but some manufacturers are fitting them because it sells cars.

The next generation of engines will be subjected to further emissions controls, and Mark Aston jokes that a Morgan might do as well as an electric car because of its lightness . . . The permitted sound level from the exhaust system is 74db in 1993, and this is monitored in the MOT test. However, Morgans average out at 75db, and the noise is from the vehicle in general, with ancillaries like the alternator and fan contributing to the exhaust noise. The Morgan's louvres let noise out which might be muffled under a regular bonnet.

DoT INSPECTIONS

There are the inspections from the Department of Transport to take into account; once a year they remove a car from dispatch and take it apart to check the build quality, and every year they come in to check the car against the type approvals. Even something like the latest wire wheel option for the Plus 8 has to receive approval. They have to satisfy braking standards, noise, 16in tyre regs, and strength of spokes. In order to sell cars abroad, documentation of this sort has to be right up to scratch. There are no less than thirty-eight individual EEC Standard type approval documents, which each foreign Morgan agent has copies of. These vary from a couple of pages about unleaded fuel to forty pages on emissions. This matrix of thirty-eight categories is updated every year, and the cars tested and inspected accordingly. Morgan can keep up by updating, and ensuring that inspectors are fully conversant with Morgan production techniques. They have to be assured that a batch of king pins or stub axles can be traced if necessary, and that quality is constantly monitored. These inspections involve looking round the factory as well as checking each model, and the manufacturer pays for the privilege. Part numbers are scrutinized which is fine for items made in-house, but outside suppliers seem to change part numbers with astonishing speed, and this has to be taken into account. It takes two months to circulate the paperwork, and even longer with the Plus 8 because the tests are done in Germany. A major player like Ford, intent on bringing out a new model such as the Mondeo, would probably take about three years to get all thirty-eight tests done.

Cars are meant to be European now, but the Belgians and French are a law unto themselves with regard to type approval legislation; seatbelt tests are a problem in Belgium where they do not recognize an interpretation specifically for sports cars. There is virtually a different version of every Morgan model for all EEC markets, let alone non-EEC countries; the Swiss update their legislation every six months. In 1995 an overall European standard will in theory mean that UK type approval is good enough. Outside the EEC it is a fickle world. The United States will not accept documentation which refers to kilometres; is this an example of protectionism rearing its ugly head again? At least this is something not permitted between EEC member states.

Back on the home front, because of outside suppliers' cutbacks or chasing new ones where they have gone out of business, Mark now works a lot with Roger Talbot who does the buying for production. He will source new suppliers for parts required on Bill Beck's prototypes. Mark also reckons now to spend 70 per cent of his time sorting out legislation issues with the various workshops;

Thanks to briefings from the SMMT, Morgan are never in the dark about forthcoming legislation.

it is a two-way matter, since the foremen will know how easily something can be implemented. Because of the EPA environmental legislation, Morgan will have to spend something like £150,000 on new equipment in the paint shop. This takes care of roughly half the company's annual profit. The new equipment will last four years, after which something else will be required; there is no telling where it will end. Complying with legislation is invariably an expensive business; to do all the emissions tests and changes on the T16 engine cost £15,000, which is offset against 120 Plus 4s a year. In five years there will be new standards. Ultimately, legislation will force the prices of the cars up. It is bad news for enthusiasts, but there is no other way. The three-way catalyst probably adds £1,000 to the price of the car, although the company absorbed all the development costs.

There is no doubt that Morgan has to be ahead of the game on legislation; thanks to the SMMT and Mark Aston's diligence in assessing what the changes will mean to Morgan, the car is now ahead of the next set of rules, and selling in the American market which is ahead of Europe. These happen to be lighting regulations, to do with angles of visibility, because all lighting surfaces on cars have to be within certain criteria. A couple of these do not conform to the impending regs; the reversing lights are too low and could not be raised sufficiently without interfering with the bumper height. The solution had to be a single light above the bumper, which was not such a tidy layout. The rear fog lamp on the four-seater has had to be moved over by an inch-and-a-quarter because it was too close to the brake light. And so it goes on.

12 Driving Experience

Not unnaturally, both Peter and Charles Morgan drive their own product – it would be surprising if they didn't – and when one is in the position of owning a car factory, one is entitled to take things to the limit; hence Charles's 'blue car', the Plus 8 with the honeycomb chassis. On the road for everyday use however, Charles uses an indigo blue Plus 8, and a Plus 4 four-seater for family motoring. He also has an older model Mercedes 200T estate as a family hack. It is important for him to drive Morgans under all circumstances, from London traffic to the Welsh hills, the lanes as well as the motorway, so that he knows what it is like to be a Morgan owner. He borrows other cars just to keep in touch with what else is available, and compares the Morgans critically with these. In spite of such drawbacks as the lack of a power hood or the noise level on a motorway journey, he believes you cannot beat a Morgan as an all-round performance car.

PLUS 4

Having been lent a Plus 4 for a week and clocked up a lot of miles in Worcestershire and Herefordshire, I am inclined to agree. I loved every minute of it, and found the Morgan totally absorbing. It involves the driver, drawing out the very best in you, urging you to refine your technique. You have to be sharp, keeping on top of every situation, which makes every mile of fast A

Naturally Charles Morgan drives his own product, and is seen here with his wife Jane on the 1992 Tour de France in BUY 600M.

Once bitten by the Morgan bug it is almost inevitable that one will join the club and want to participate in events such as this sprint at Curborough.

or B road interesting to drive. Steering is so direct and the car responds instantly to whatever you tell it to do. It demands commitment, for the moment you relax and your mind wanders, it will catch you out. Every mile in a Morgan is a major event, frequently entertaining, sometimes thrilling, and always engrossing as you are concentrating on making it go where you want it to. It is also a forgiving car, being easy to get back into shape if you do go into a bend too quickly. This kind of motoring is wholly refreshing, a breath of fresh air to senses dulled by decades of modernity; even my regular spirited Alfa Romeo motoring seemed a doddle compared with the discipline required by the Morgan. Back at the wheel of my 3.0-litre Alfa 75 I thought I was in charge of a bag of cotton wool. But such intense concentration can be tiring too, and if one wanted to be critical of the Morgan, it is this aspect which is its one drawback: the

highs and lows are incessant. At least in the Alfa I can switch off if I want to. I suppose in an ideal world one would have the Morgan as a second car for high days and holidays, although this is no doubt heresy to seasoned Morgan stalwarts. The following reflections will not surprise these ascetics, but may be of interest to anyone who has yet to experience the Morgan phenomenon.

Getting into your Morgan may frustrate the uninitiated, the corpulent, or like me someone more familiar with an Alfa Spider or somesuch; that is because it is a bit tight between door, steering wheel, seat and side panel. I can only say that you get used to it and develop a knack of levering yourself in and out. If your car has no exterior door handles, you have to slide the perspex window forward to gain access to the inner handle. For me, this would place exterior handles high on my specification list. There may be advantages of weight saving,

This is the development Plus 4 which the author was lent for a few days, and forms the basis for many of the comments made in this chapter. It stands beside the wood shed where planks of sawn ash are stored, and a couple of treated frames can be seen.

aerodynamics even, but trying to slide the window open on a frosty morning tends rather to mitigate against having no outside handles.

Once installed in the driving seat and comforted by the heady smell of leather, you find yourself relatively close to the upright steering wheel, which is always in contact with your thighs. Your legs are stretched out ahead of you, with none of that splayed knees nonsense of Alfa Romeos. There are two seat styles; bucket or the thicker, reclining type, with the latter standard in the four-seater. A new seat with a much more wrap-around feel to it is in the offing. I tried one for size in Charles Morgan's blue Plus 8 and thought it would have to be my choice. The regular bucket seat has a hard, supportive back, although a bit vague as far as the squab is concerned. There is no space for your left foot in a right-hand drive car, so inevitably you find it resting gently on the clutch pedal. Your right calf is supported nicely by the inside of the scuttle.

A Morgan tells you what is happening to it, which accounts for much of its success as a competition car. Whereas many racing cars can dish out the performance, they do not respond with much feel; the Morgan is quite the opposite, especially if it is a competition car with its suspension tied down harder than normal. This allows the driver literally to feel the chassis flexing with the seat of his pants and the brakes gripping through the steering wheel. The solid back axle, leaf springs and sliding pillar front end generate the tactile qualities of the Morgan, and to replace or in some way update them would be to reduce the feel of the car. Ironically the car which won the Morgan Championship in 1992 was the least modified of the lot.

Attempting a tricky reversing manoeuvre in a 1980 Plus 8 during an autotest at Elvaston Castle.

RUMBLING POWER: THE PLUS 8

If one was to drive a brand-new Plus 8, followed by one from seven years ago, and then a twenty-year-old example, it would be a salutary lesson in Morgan evolution, as they would feel like totally different cars. The current car would feel more powerful, the steering lighter, it would be more compliant, the shock absorbers quicker to react, brakes sharper, and the car would be much quieter, due to the catalyst. And it would hold together better.

Peter Morgan is a bit of a Ferrari fan, and keeps his 4.4-litre 365 GT 2+2 under wraps in dispatch; it does not come out very often now, but he very kindly lent me his latest Plus 8 for a couple of days to compare with the Plus 4. What a beast! Its 3.9-litre engine takes it into another realm, with massive power always on tap at the merest dab of the throttle. Unless you drive this kind of car all

the time, acceleration is breathtaking, such is its power-to-weight ratio, and not much else on the road can live with it. Bends are straightened out, and on a familiar road, where you normally thought there was not room to overtake, a prod on the Plus 8's accelerator has you blasting past the slow-coaches. When the V8 was roaring into its stride at 4,500rpm it took me straight back twenty years to watching Formula 5000 or Group 7 CanAm cars thundering round Brands Hatch. The aura of the V8 is considerable. But that is not the whole story. I was almost as equally impressed by the car's docile qualities. It will happily trundle along at 1,500rpm in top, doing around 40mph (65km/h) in a stream of traffic, its scarcely muted rumble hinting at potential performance and turning heads everywhere. Because of the enormous reservoir of power, it is not necessary to drive it as quickly as possible all the time, and I feel that this makes the Plus 8 a much better touring car than the Plus 4 or 4/4. Aside from the consideration of luggage space which affects all two-seaters, it would not be so tiring.

But try your hand at a winding hillclimb like the one near Teddington (on the B4077) near Stow-on-the-Wold in the Cotswolds, and you have pause for thought. Thanks to the Plus 8, I discovered what a dreadful surface this demanding section of road has, and I found myself hanging on for dear life! It developed into quite a wrestling match as the car bucked and jolted like a wild animal, and I decided it was behaviour best abandoned for smoother conditions. But get a Plus 8 fired up on a sweeping traffic-free A or B road, and for anyone interested in driving as an art it is nothing short of a life-enhancing experience!

If your car is one of the latest generation with a catalyst, you will find you cannot fill up with anything but unleaded at the pumps, because only the smaller nozzle can get down the filler pipe. Once up and running, one of the first things you notice when setting out for a drive in a Morgan is the sharp clutch; you do not notice the roller-pedal for the accelerator, which I once imagined might be a little odd. There is no brake servo to help out with retardation, so you need to press hard. It is as well to remember this if an emergency looms. All Morgans have the fly-off handbrake, and although I can appreciate the merits of it, I assume that their operation is a knack, as on both cars I tried, it was a matter of trial and error as to whether it worked or not. Best to leave the car in gear when parking it. The gear lever is right next to the steering wheel, beautifully placed, and the shift is tight and notchy. You sit right up against the steering wheel, leather-rimmed these days, with no space between wheel and thighs; you feel like Dick Seaman rather than Stirling Moss, getting those biceps working at low speeds. No straight arm, flicking wrist action here! In fact you control a Plus 8 with almost every part of your body, which makes it a sexy, sensory sort of car.

There is no better car for blowing away the cobwebs and getting back to nature.

Once out on the open road, there is a real thrill looking down that long bonnet with all its louvres. Torpedo sidelights on the wings indicate the car's periphery, which helps in tight spaces. Running at night, the sidelights cast a comfortable glow against the wings, headlights and the side of the bonnet. Conversely, the main beam warning light is a mite bright, although the lights themselves are very effective. I used the Plus 8's spotlights at night and think that on balance you could probably justify having them, provided they are properly aligned; but there is nothing wrong with the regular headlights in the normal course of things. Three wipers take care of any precipitation; funnily enough you never really notice the peculiarity of the middle blade, introduced with the Plus 8's shallower windscreen. The wood-veneer dashboard of the Plus 8 stood proud of the normal dash, so that the column-mounted wiper switch was against it; it did not affect its operation though. Unlike the majority of Morgans, apart from the Moss-gearbox Plus 8, the new Plus 4 lever is straight rather than crooked.

There is a bit of wind noise from the hood, which increases with velocity. At constant high speed it can be wearing; Charles remembers driving a borrowed Plus 8 fitted with a fibreglass hard-top, and being surprised to discover he was driving quite normally at 120mph (190km/h). The hard-top was so well insulated that it cut out the wind noise, so the aural sensation did not match the speed. The wind noise can therefore be seen as beneficial as far as one's driving licence is concerned, since it is a natural inhibitor of very high speeds! I discovered that in heavy rain you get drips coming down from the extreme corners of the screen, and it was a case of the faster you go the greater the flow. This may not be a general thing, of course, and you are probably so involved with driving that you fail to notice your leg getting damp.

Another fascinating little quirk is that when driving through rain, the layout of the wings is such that you can watch the water flicking off the tyres when lock is applied. To eliminate rain ingress from the side windows you tuck a weather strip over the outside of the window frame. Everything was much tauter on the newer Plus 8 than on the well-used Plus 4. When driving with the top up, as one would tend to do in the depths of winter, the view is cut off just above eye level by the top of the screen and the sides of the hood. So if you fancy glancing at the scenery you are obliged to crouch in your seat and peer under the hood.

CONCLUSION

So is the Morgan a machine for the masochist? The revised rear damper layout has made for a more supple ride, and in general I found little to complain about on poor road surfaces. It used to be said that Morgans were only good so long as the road surface was billiard-table smooth, like most race tracks, otherwise the marbles and pot-holes would toss the car this way and that in a similar way to that which I described earlier. But then I only found the one piece of road bad enough to experience this.

However, you do put up with a few disadvantages like a lack of luggage space for the enjoyment of a two-seater Morgan, but you say cheerio to bland hot-hatch mediocrity and have lots of fun. Many of us have forgotten the thrills of open-air motoring, the all-round visibility, the keenness of sights and sounds, tempered by the fumes if you are unlucky enough to get stalled in a jam. A lot of the fun of an open car is to do with stimulation of the senses, proximity to the road, to the scenery, the evocative noise of the Plus 8 rumble. The Plus 4 makes up for a rather dull noise from its T16 twin-cam by providing reliable torque low down the

Driving a Morgan fast tends to make the hood billow slightly at the sides, demonstrated by Charles Morgan in MMC 11 at Donington in 1978.

rev range: at 2,000rpm in top it will be doing 50mph (80km/h), with oil pressure at 60psi. Curiously for a fuel-injected engine, it emits a sucking noise as if it was on carburettors. The gruff 2.0-litre lump provides gutsy, torquey performance. You come to realize that it will not let you down when overtaking, that it will keep on accelerating when you need it to. Up around 80mph (130km/h)

when the wind noise has become intrusive, the Plus 4 becomes a demanding but enthralling mistress on a winding road. Few things are more rewarding than getting a succession of sweeping bends just right; up around 90–100mph (145–160km/h), it really comes into its own, and you are so busy you do not notice the external din. These are surely the reasons for having one.

13 The Workforce

At Morgan everyone is very much aware that they produce a special product, which gives the company an edge in the viciously competitive world of the automotive industry. Special factors apart from the build quality are the levels of performance, reliability and durability, and ease of maintenance in foreign markets, lack of attention to which has probably killed off many small manufacturers over the years. Witness abandoned Maseratis in Australia, or Alfas dumped in the US. Interestingly, Morgan is the only motor manufacturer never to have got into serious financial difficulties, and uniquely, it has managed to remain in the control of the family which founded it. The workforce of 130 is made up of nineteen in administration and 111 in building the cars. All manual workers are very well trained, having for the most part started off with the company and come straight from school or technical college at Worcester or Kidderminster. This skilled body of men and a few women is drawn locally from Malvern, Ledbury and Worcester, and over the years has remained loyal to the business through the odd financial crisis or national dispute. Peter Morgan recalls that a few workers once walked out for a couple of days as a token gesture for the local branch of the engineering union when a national stoppage was taking place. He was referring to the three-day week.

Several fathers and sons are currently employed. The hierarchy of Peter Morgan, Chairman and Managing Director, and his son Charles, Production Manager, is one such example of course. Both go into the factory every day, and strategically, Peter

Peter Morgan, the figurehead of the company.

remains the man everyone looks up to and seeks advice from. He is often accompanied by Jade, his rough-haired collie, who wanders round the stores area and is a sort of factory mascot. Charles joined in 1984 when he was 33, abandoning a promising career as an ITV film cameraman; he had just finished filming Sandy Gall with the Mujahedin behind the Russian lines in Afghanistan, and narrowly escaped a low-level bombing run by a Russian Mig; appearing on the Morgan stand at the Earls Court Motor Show must have seemed a little tame if rather more secure! By any standards, his career seems little short of intrepid: a shot at the Cresta Run, ice-racing in a Morgan at St Moritz, Production Sports Car Champion in 1978, and a newsreel cameraman in places like the Lebanon and Kampuchea. He still keeps his hand in on the competition front.

There is a board of six directors, including Peter and Charles Morgan, Jane Morgan, Heather Morgan (Peter's wife), Works Manager and Assistant Managing Director Mark Aston, Sales Director Derek Day, and Company Secretary Geoff Margetts. Roughly two or three new employees are taken on each year, so that there may be eight or so in training at any given time; all are committed Morgan fans from the outset. There used to be a six-year apprenticeship, now down to four years, which includes day release at technical college, and the trainee comes out with City and Guilds HNDs. He or she will then specialize in whichever department has been opted for. This is in addition to the training given by each of the shop foremen at the factory, who will have various jobs he can introduce the trainee to. Inevitably some will want to specialize in a particular aspect of the car's production, but they are dissuaded from this early on in order to get an all-round training and to avoid them getting in a rut. After training, it is normal for an employee to stick to the one chosen workshop. It struck me that everyone involved in the different stages of Morgan production works at a brisk pace, with something verging on slickness. In fact I was mildly surprised to see craftsmen in the wood or trim shops going so fast with such precision.

Foremen prefer Morgan-trained employees rather than those who have learned their trade elsewhere, as their work is particularly specialized. There is quite a finely balanced line between having exactly the right number of staff and being understaffed. If too many trainees are at college, or a 'flu bug takes its toll, or the pre-Christmas rush to get holiday allocation used up has removed too great a number of Morgan employees, shop foremen start to get

The staff of the repair shop relax on old car seats during their tea break; here they pretend to look serious in contrast to the normal jovial proceedings.

Development Engineer Bill Beck often initiates ideas for the future and wants to see as many items standardized as possible for ease of production.

Assistant Managing Director and Works Manager Mark Aston has the onerous task of relating automotive legislation to Morgan production.

Mark Baldwin is foreman of the repair shop, and following in his father's footsteps, he joined the firm in 1983 taking charge in 1990.

Geoff Brewer joined Morgan in 1955, and here he is supervising the repanelling of MMC 11, Charles Morgan and Rob Wells' racing car.

Foreman Graham Hall, who joined Morgan in 1953, (pictured here with door components) has been closely involved with the evolution of the frame, and spends much of his time making new jigs.

Trim shop foreman Charlie Styles keeps a stock of standard shades of leather, but since it takes four hides to upholster a two-seater, other colours have to be ordered from Connolly's in advance.

There is an excellent cameraderie among the workforce, with numerous ongoing small wagers such as the betting on the arrival of 'first snow' chalked on the wall.

worried. A few men can be moved from one department to another if production efficiency is threatened. Stocktaking is one time when foremen at least are under pressure, when every single item in the shop is counted, which must be fun in the machine shop where they get down to nuts and bolts. This takes place during one of the two weeks' annual holiday shut-down. When a foreman takes his holiday, he must ensure all stocks are in the pipeline for the vehicles which will be built during his absence.

The Morgan factory operates on a 39-hour five-day week, with overtime built into the weekdays. Until 1992 the men were able to do 4½ hours' overtime on Saturday, but this left many feeling that the weekend had passed them by. So it was agreed at pay negotiations in spring 1992 that the lunch break would be reduced to half an hour and the working day would end at 5.30pm instead of 5.00pm, apart from Fridays, when the men finish at 4.00pm. The factory would re-open at 8.00am on Monday. This neat arrangement brought the production time up to scratch, and everyone was happy as they had a full weekend.

UNION MEMBERSHIP

About 50 per cent of the workforce belongs

to a union: but just to create confusion, there are nine different unions! Not surprisingly, in the tin shop it is the Sheet Metal and Boilermakers Trade Federation. It is not quite a closed shop; the tin shop has tried to operate such a regime for many years, and it is a question of every new employee being signed up. Now there are a few employees there who belong to a different union. There are TGWU, Engineering Workers Union and a number of others. But wage negotiations now take place in discussions throughout the factory, rather than with the department concerned, which is how it used to be done. There were once eighteen different negotiators involving union and non-union workers, but now there are just three representatives for the whole factory, and once a general agreement is reached with them, the deal is passed on to the rest of the workforce.

There has never been any significant union action at the factory. Occasionally there has been a personal matter where an individual has sought union backing, although there was a strike during the three-day week in 1974. The union called for compliance, and when non-union personnel carried on working, there was some trouble. But when a poll was taken amongst other motor manufacturers and it was found that most were ignoring the union directive, the strikers returned to work. It was all over in a matter of four days.

PAY STRUCTURE

The pay structure at the factory is a curious one. Each department is paid according to productivity, on a system that is built into all wage agreements. There are several different systems; some of the shops operate on piece-work basis, where the pay system is very complicated although rationalized a few years ago when Geoff Margetts took over as Company Secretary. The system is complicated because of the varied nature of what each department produces, but happily it is largely self-regulating. The shops that are producing individual bits and pieces, like the machine shop and sheet metal shop, tend to work on a piece-work basis, making a certain number of objects per hour, not necessarily linked to the whole vehicle (even producing body panels), and they are paid at an hourly rate.

Some departments work on a bonus-scheme basis, where they are paid by the car as it is difficult to quantify the individual work they are doing because of the variations involved. The wiring or trim shop have lots of different operations on the go, but all linked to a particular car. This could be separated out so they were paid on a piece-work basis, but as it is, they are paid for complete cars, with however many variations, produced during the period of a week. So in fact the shop is paid an overall sum of money which is divided accordingly between people who work there. Some of the individual items like hood and tonneau cover, for instance, have a specific price, which goes into the pool and is split between them. The trim shop will earn more for a car upholstered in leather than for one in PVC Ambla because there is more labour involved and the material is dearer. In the paint shop, restorations and touch-ups are calculated by the hour, whereas painting a car is done on a car by car basis. The benefit of operating a system like this is that it makes the employees encourage one another to maintain progress and keep things rolling. It is down to the foreman to understand the production targets and the arithmetic of the system in order to cope with the pool of timesheets, which not only indicate what the department is owed, but serve as check-lists for which cars have passed through the department.

There used to be a cost of living payment

Norman Henton, who has worked at Morgan for forty-six years, is preparing a spindle moulder jig for scuttle rail ends. On the racks behind him are assorted jigs and sections of wood for the frame.

Paint Shop foreman Derek Gardner is delighted if customers choose unusual colours, but most stick to the traditional range.

Each person has to be responsible for his part in the build process, and there is always consultation whenever a problem occurs, so that assembly is completed correctly.

which was paid in with the wages, but this unearned addition was detrimental to the bonus and discouraged the incentive to make extra. This has now been eroded by wage settlements, which was not regarded as an entirely popular move by those who saw themselves short at the end of a bad week.

It took a long time to get the workforce to accept that they could produce the extra tenth car a week. They were persuaded by a financial incentive for the tenth car. But now, a couple of years later, they are worried if it looks as if only nine cars will be finished. Speeding up production of particular parts is only relevant if it happens at every stage, and then it is of doubtful value, resulting in lapses in quality with jobs left undone, and at the worst, cars sitting in fields. Elimination of waste is more important, according to Charles Morgan. This means getting the car right first time, particularly in the area of paintwork; if a car has to have any part of its paintwork redone, it means a big delay.

COMMUNICATION

To an extent, Morgan manufacture is both diplomatic and co-operative. Any change made to the cars is done in consultation with the shop floor, to get the opinions and reactions of everybody involved with the manufacture. There is no hint of a communication problem at Morgan, as foremen are often to be seen in discussion with each other, and other employees circulate either socially or in the course of their work. In the past, the development shop would come up with a new idea, present it to the shop floor and expect them to get on and build it. But the concept may have been flawed for some reason clear to the shop floor but not to the development shop. Nowadays the three people involved in design and development work closely with the shop floor. I met Development Engineer Bill Beck during a tea break in the repair shop, where most of the work is carried out on experimental systems. This seemed to exemplify the excellent relations between the different departments and the workforce

Amiable card school in progress in the tin shop during the half-hour lunch break.

Taking a break from trimming, the lunch break provides an opportunity for some card play.

in general. The tea break is sacrosanct: even the blaring of Radio 1 is temporarily silenced while people do crosswords, play cards, eat sandwiches, joke and gossip. The

inter-departmental harmony is such that two years ago, a factory team pulled a Plus 8 around the county on a bank holiday to raise money for a scanner. Working in teams of

There is a good deal of social interaction during break times; these craftsmen and women work in different departments and meet up for a chat and a cup of tea.

ten at a time, they raised £7,776, and in what smacks of latter-day highway robbery, were actually to be seen halting oncoming traffic to relieve the drivers of small change! Another extramural factory activity which seems to have gone by the board now is the football team which flourished until the neighbouring firm took back a corner of the pitch, which did apparently belong to them. There are small ongoing wagers within the factory, such as betting on when the first snow of the winter will arrive; the dates are chalked up on the walls here and there and provide a record of local meteorology.

Part of the Morgan factory philosophy is that each person is accountable for his or her actions, as this is seen as fundamental to successful production; a job is not passed on down the line unless it is done correctly, because it will simply be stalled at the next stage. Quality is thus controlled by the workforce, but in general I came across only people who enjoyed what they were doing and took pride in doing it well.

Customer input is considered important too. Everyone wants to personalize his Morgan, and all the traditional appendages like bonnet straps are still asked for. Iconoclastic safety legislation has caused some of these gems to be removed, like the Norton filler cap, a period flick-off brass affair which could not pass the fumes test because vapour has to be filtered through a charcoal canister to the atmosphere. At the moment only modern plastic caps can cope with the pressure, although such is the customer demand for the re-introduction of the Norton cap that Morgan may have it made with an appropriate pressure valve and bring it back.

14 The Market-place

You might think that the sales office of a firm with an order book full for six or seven years ahead might be taking things easy, resting on its laurels rather. At Morgan this is anything but the case. The indefatigable Sales Director Derek Day and his assistant Mark Reed appear never to stop beavering away. They are frequently called to the phone over the factory tannoy, breaking up a discussion with a workshop foreman about a query over some component in a

Sales Director Derek Day (right), *and Assistant Sales Director Mark Read double as Morgan's public relations officers as well as keeping in constant touch with agents, customers and workforce.*

customer's specification. Or they might be discussing delivery dates with agents, then helping a potential customer decide which model to choose, and what may be the most appropriate extras for his intended use.

They double as the company's press and public relations office, especially if Charles Morgan is busy, fielding queries and doing interviews. Then they will have to escort customers and visitors around the factory. One of the great things about Morgan is the openness to visitors. Virtually anyone who is seriously interested in the company can book to make a factory visit. For many it is literally a pilgrimage, a journey back to the birthplace of their pride and joy; in the cream tongue and groove panelled reception room, with its framed posters and illustrations depicting Morgan exploits, is a visitor's book, with addresses from all over the world testifying to many foreign visitors. Its signatures are those of owners, some of whose cars are in build, potential customers, and students of the motor industry.

As when you order anything, you speak first to the salesman. To order your Morgan you start off with a letter to Derek or Mark, or your favourite Morgan agent. You get a letter back saying 'Thanks a lot, we will be able to do something in about five years or so'. It is always an approximate delivery schedule, but at least you are now in the queue. There is even an endowment arrangement with a finance house which you can pay into while you wait. About six months before your letter comes to the top of the pile, Derek Day will write asking you for a £500 deposit. The next step is to decide exactly what car you want, and what extras

you would like on it. Derek will prepare the legendary build ticket, which specifies what is to be built and what add-ons are required, copies of which are attached to the car at every stage of the process. Then you will be notified when things have got under way. Sometimes a customer will decide to change his specification when production of the car has started. Derek has to be fairly strict about keeping people tied down to whatever has been agreed and is written on the build ticket, otherwise chaos would ensue. Of the waiting list, Derek Day says there must be a cut-off point beyond which people will not be prepared to wait. So far they have not been tested on that. I would imagine it might be ten years; I could not envisage hanging on for longer than that. Besides, Peter Morgan will not commit himself to speculating about any scenario further ahead than five years, so in a way, why should his customers?

Foreign agents have customers asking for cars in the summertime, which Morgan just cannot allow for. From the factory's point of view, it is obviously far better to make a steady nine or ten cars a week all year round rather than dash off twenty a week during the summer to satisfy fair-weather drivers, even if it were possible. As a result of the perilous situation Morgan found itself in when the US market slumped in recession in the mid-sixties, the company has since aimed at a worldwide market rather than just one country. Only the Plus 8 goes to the US now, but at least it conforms to Federal standards and no longer has to run on propane. Derek is proud of the fact that Italians, noted for charismatic supercars, and Japanese, who are at the forefront of automotive innovation, are keen to buy Morgans, and that there is a keen following for the marque in these countries. To get the volumes into perspective, about 50 per cent of Morgan's annual production, say 230 cars, is exported, and the Japanese are taking thirty new cars a year, so whilst the numbers are not shattering, they are significant for Morgan. The Germans will have as many Morgans as the

---

Morgan Price List 1993

4/4 1600 two-seater	£13,220	Plus 8-type spotlights (pair)	£65
4/4 1600 two-seater	£14,520	Reversing lights	£60
(Plus 4 body style)		Pleated rear seats	£75
4/4 1600 four-seater	£14,325	(four-seater only)	
4/4 1600 four-seater	£15,625		
(Plus 4 body style)		**Extras Applicable to all Models**	
Plus 4 two-seater	£16,300	Badge bar	£30
Plus 4 four-seater	£17,515	Towing bracket	£60
Plus 8 petrol injection 3.9-litre	£21,190	Towing bracket complete with	£135
		electrics	

Extras

Plus 8

Leather upholstery, Connolly	£650	Door handles	£52.50
HB/PAC grade (black and		Bonnet strap	£32.50
certain colours)		Undersealing	£95
Leather upholstery, Connolly	£750	Rustproofing	£180
Autolux grade		Aluminium body and wings	£450
Leather upholstery, Connolly	£825	Dual tone paintwork	£315
Autolux grade (white,		Special colour paintwork	£50
magnolia and special colours)		Metallic paintwork	£235
Reclining and folding seats	£150	Coloured hood, sidescreens,	
Luggage carrier	£125	tonneau	
		Two-seater	£175
		Four-seater	£265

4/4 and Plus 4

Wire wheels chromium plated	£350	Rivenhood hood, sidescreens,	
(4/4 only)		tonneau	
Wire wheels chromium plated	£375	Two-seater	£700
(Plus 4 only)		Four-seater	£920
Leather upholstery, Connolly		Spare wheel cover	£50
HB/PAC grade		Head restraints	£110
Two-seater (black and certain	£595	Walnut veneered facia board	£190
colours)		Galvanized chassis	£160
Four-seater (black and certain	£735	Passenger door mirror	£25
colours)		Extra wing tread rubbers	£32.50
Leather upholstery, Connolly		Organ-type accelerator pedal	£25
Autolux grade		Coloured carpets	£75
Two-seater	£695	Cigar lighter	£30
Four-seater	£835	Map reading light	£35
Leather upholstery, Connolly		Clock	£70
Autolux grade		Four-seater windscreen fitted onto	£10
Two-seater (white, magnolia	£770	two-seater	
and specials)		Speakers and aerial	£80
Four-seater (white, magnolia	£910	Radio-cassette players, quoted on	
and specials)		request	
Luggage carrier, two-seater	£125		
Luggage carrier, four-seater	£150		
Reclining and folding seats	£150		
(two-seater only)			

The Morgan price list and extras available in 1993. Prices are ex-works, exclusive of tax. It is interesting to note the relative values placed on items which may in turn enhance the comfort, appearance and longevity of your car.

factory will allow them, and the flourishing Italian Morgan club issues a very sophisticated pictorial annual brochure. It is a very classy production.

Orders come from such unlikely places as Poland, Greenland and Iceland, Cyprus and Turkey, and as I talked to him Derek was in negotiations with a customer from Czechoslovakia. Customers from France, Denmark and Luxembourg were due in the same week. He is a strong believer in the car being its own best advert, saying 'Once you can get a car into a market, that market will develop.' He endorses the problems of legislation in selling cars in different markets, and believes the Single European Market is perhaps five years away; it certainly did not start on 1 January 1993.

TRADITIONALIST OWNERS

Derek Day joined Morgan straight from school in 1947, making him the longest-serving employee. He has done almost all the jobs on the admin side at one time or another, having started off as office boy, tea-maker, telephonist and receptionist, and got to know the cars through handling spares and taking people round the factory. He was subsequently appointed Sales Manager and then a Director. As far as the customers' preferences are concerned, he remembers that in the early 1950s, most people wanted cream, ivory or red. These colours are still popular of course, even though the shades have changed, but they have been overtaken by the Connaught green. As one can see in the paint and trim departments, there are colour schemes chosen by individualists such as ivory and black or two-tone silver but, confirms Derek, 'Nowadays the traditionalist will only have red or green'. But the more exotic colours do not generally get used every day; they are usually for high days and holidays. And probably Morgans are bought as second, third or even fourth cars

The sales department constantly monitors the progress of every car, ensuring that the specification is adhered to; here Dan Monk checks the brakes before delivery.

181

Morgan Clubs

Few makes of car inspire such commitment and devotion on the part of their owners. Just as there are agents all over the world, so there are flourishing Morgan clubs, meeting regularly for competitions, socials, concours, and 'noggins', the more informal get-togethers. Closest to home of the foreign clubs is the Morgan Sports Car Club of Holland, which in addition to a host of social events, organizes driving tests at Zandvoort circuit. Also in Europe, Morgan Club Italia takes advantage of Monza to put on club driving sessions. Founded in 1981, the club's annual brochure is a very sophisticated production, and there are the obvious outings to Tuscany. The Swiss club has been going a little longer, since 1977 in fact, and there is the added bonus of wonderful Alpine and Jura scenery to their meetings. The Spanish club is nearly ten years old now, and members were inspired by a Plus 8 seen in the hands of that keen motorist, King Juan Carlos. Scandinavians have clubs in Norway and Denmark, and the Morgan Owners' Group of Sweden, with a wide variety of cars amongst its membership, built up since 1966. There are local meetings and two main events, in spring and autumn. Germany has two centres, at Cologne and Baden, and there are clubs in Austria, France and Belgium, which has two. Pol-Mog, the Polish club, is somewhat limited to summer meetings by virtue of the climate. Cypriot members are naturally unaffected in this way.

There are no less than eleven Morgan clubs in the United States, which gives an idea of the depth of feeling that the cars provoke. Over in the west are the two Californian Plus 4 Clubs, Northern and Southern; these were founded in 1957 and 1955 respectively, with the former growing out of the other's San Francisco chapter. There are events run jointly by both clubs, including races at Laguna Seca. Other clubs are in Texas, the North-West, Ohio, where restorations take high priority, Philadelphia, with a strong three-wheeler contingent; the Great Lakes boasts the club mag with the most unusual title: *The Flexible Flyer*. In New York there is the 3/4 Morgan Group, which hosts the usual club events throughout the warmer months, and further inland there is the Western New York Morgan Owners' Group.

Elsewhere in the world, growing Japanese interest in the cars is channelled into the club headquarters in Tokyo, with five provincial centres, meeting up near Mount Fuji for the annual bash. Also in the Far East, Morgans are well represented in Hong Kong. Top-up motoring is frowned upon by the club in New Zealand, whilst considerations of distance seem not to deter owners in South Africa from getting together. Back home, the Morgan Sports Car Club reaches members with the lively *Miscellany* magazine, a mixture of technical tips, members' anecdotes and adverts. There are news bulletins from the 30 regional centres which have names like SmogMog for London or SpotMog for Gloucestershire. Peter Morgan is President, and Chris Rowe is the editor of *Miscellany*. Registrar is Christine Healey, 41, Cordwell Close, Castle Donington, Derbyshire, DE74 2JL.

now. People categorize their car buying by price as well as by model, and surprisingly, some customers do look at the competition before coming to Morgan. I should have thought it was such a specific choice that nothing else would do. Once a customer's car is under way, Derek is immediately involved with scheduling its progress. He cannot simply sit back and direct operations, as it is largely down to him to pull the car through the factory to the approximate delivery date he gave the customer. All aspects of the procedure have to be monitored and the customer usually wants to be kept informed. The monitoring is not because of any weakness in the workshops. It is a fail-safe precaution, because every car is different. From time to time a couple will coincide of course, and there are plenty in Connaught green with black leather trim. But there will

Final polish in the dispatch bay before delivery.

almost always be variations. 'Our strength here is being able to have this contact with the customer and with the workforce,' says Derek. 'That's the way it's got to be, because that's partly what sells Morgans.'

There is usually a strong bond between Morgan owners and the factory, and the repair shop carries out any after-sales servicing that is needed. 'This rapport between factory and customer is what helps persuade them to have another Morgan,' maintains Derek. 'A lot of garages are happy to sell a car but don't want to know if anything goes wrong with it; but that's not us!' Only a small number of owners bring their cars back to the factory for servicing, for obvious geographical reasons, but go instead to their nearest Morgan representative. Agents are allocated cars more or less on a chronological basis, so that an agent with only a handful of cars on order will still have to wait in turn to fulfil orders alongside one with perhaps forty in hand. Derek admits to a little bit of juggling to accommodate the busiest agencies, but in general it will not help you to ring round to find someone with only a few cars on order!

Fortunately Morgans do not depreciate, which means the second-hand market is buoyant. And if the second-hand market is healthy, it creates a market for new cars. On the subject of profiteering, Charles had this to say: 'We would like to think all our customers are magnificent people; but when one of them sells his order on for an extra one or two thousand pounds, which we see none of, we wonder, well was he a very nice customer for a Morgan or what? No, he was a speculator!' The recession has at least cleared them out; whereas the boom-time premium might have been as much as £7,000 on a new Morgan, now it is down to about £1,000. If a person placed his order in order to speculate, and found when his car came up for build that the market was depressed, he would probably cancel. If Derek Day suspected the car was going to be moved on immediately it was built, he would simply ensure that the deposit was secure and the car was registered in the customer's name. At the height of the mid to late eighties boom, a lot of cars were ordered

MORGAN MODELS

There were several three-wheelers including 1/43 die-casts of the Darmont by Brumm from the late seventies and early eighties, and these are still relatively common. Before the war you could make your own out of Meccano, whilst other post-war offerings were by Gakken, Riko, Minicraft and Acorn. In more sophisticated white metal die-cast are 1/43 1932 Super Sports and 1/24 Super Sports from 1934 by South Eastern, (formerly Wills) Finecast. At the time of writing, these cost £41.40 for the larger model and £13.95 for the smaller one. There are a couple of 1/76 kits of the 1928 Aero Supersports and 1933 Super Sports by Scalelink and A.B.S. at £5.50 for the kit, and a 1/72 1939 F4 by B.K.L. Autoreplica, also at £5.50.

Four-wheelers in white metal die-cast at 1/43 scale include examples from Western Models, who did a flat-rad Plus 4 in the mid-eighties; there was a Plus 4 Plus by Motorkits, a 1962 Le Mans Plus 4 by Grand Prix, and a 1938 Le Mans 4/4 by Mikansue; Andre Marie Ruf produced a 4/4 four-seater, and Metal 43 offered the identical model. B.K.L. Autoreplica have the biggest list and the majority are still available. They are priced at £17.50 in kit form or £31.50 made up. They are a 1980s Plus 8, a 1960–1980 4/4 four-seater, a 1963 Plus 4 Plus, a 1950 4/4 flat-rad drophead coupé, a 1946 4/4 with Standard Special engine, and two- or four-seater versions of the 1938 4/4 with Coventry Climax engine. The same firm also makes a 1960–1980 cowled-rad two-seater, available as a kit for £5.50 and also a 1979 4/4 two- or four-seater in 1/24 scale. The bonnet lifts off revealing the detailed Ford Kent engine. This comes as a kit for £61.00, or built by Ken Hill for £135.00. Photo-etched wire wheels can be fitted for another £30.00. Also in 1/24 is an excellent Plus 8 by Southern Finecast, and there used to be a Metal 24 model of a Plus 8, which is no longer produced.

Then you get into plastic, but there is not much currently available. Polistil made a die-cast ready-made Plus 8 roadster and a competition version in 1/16 scale, and there were similar L/S Motorised electric kit Plus 8s of the same size. Ken Hill still has a limited stock of the Polistil cars for £13.75. At approximately 1/20, there was a novelty friction-drive two-seater Morgan by Masudaya, containing a nodding Disney figure such as Mickey Mouse, Donald Duck or Goofy. Slightly lower down the cringe-scale was a Hong Kong produced copy of this by Aremontoir, where a helmeted driver was mercifully substituted for the cartoon character. Acorn models also made a Morgan in die-cast plastic at 1/43 around 1969, and Ken Hill described a Plus 4 of unknown provenance he found in Norway; the incongruity was a large embossed figure 8 on the bonnet.

Die-cast metal toys at roughly 1/57 scale have been more plentiful, but only two are available

Superb detailing on 1/24 scale Plus 8 available in 1993, by Southern Finecast.

The Morgan Model Company offers a pedal car based on a 1956 high-cowl 4/4; prices start at £595; two-tone finish and extras are available.

now. These are the Majorette 4/4 cowled radiator at an extremely reasonable £0.95, and the Siku Plus 8 at £1.50. Others now obsolete, were Plus 8s from Tomica, one of which had the Miss Piggy Muppet driving, Tomy, Old Timer Models, Zee, and the same model by Dynawheels, Corgi Rockets, Wizz-wheels, and L/B Models. A very basic plastic 4/4 with magnetic drive was made in Czechoslovakia in the late sixties, and a 1/24 scale Plus 8 existed as a tin-plate toy.

The children's pedal cars I mentioned earlier are still very much available and are made by the Morgan Model Company. They are good reproductions in 1/3 scale of a high-cowl four-seater 4/4 *circa* 1956, made of colour-impregnated GRP mounted on a steel chassis. Each one is individually numbered, and features include battery-powered headlights and horn, fold-flat windscreen, and leather bonnet strap. There are solid rubber tyres and aluminium bumpers. Length is approximately 48in (125cm), and colours more or less echo the real thing, ranging from BRG and red to blue, yellow and white. You can even specify two-tone finish, or the Special Edition which has a number of extras like flashing indicators and working rear lights. Finally, there are a pair of silver-plated pewter Morgans in 1/57 scale, mounted on polished wooden plinths, by Mark Models. They are a Super Sports three-wheeler and a Plus 8, and can be ordered from Janet Hill Ventures, price £19.95. If you really want to stretch the Morgan models concept, what about the soap-on-a-string Plus 8 sold by Marks and Spencers, or a Plus 8 in glass crystal, or wooden representations of three-wheeler tourer and racer and a flat radiator four-wheeler by Line Nine Design? The Morgan factory actually produced a pair of 1/57 scale models recently. Remember the church pews I saw in the wood store? I was given a sneak preview of the finished stalls, resplendent in stain and beeswax polish, by foreman Graham Hall before they left the wood shop for Peter Morgan's parish church. There on the central feet were models of a Plus 8 and a 4/4, carved by Graham and looking fabulous. Like medieval misericords today, there will doubtless be much debate in centuries to come about who made them and why.

Further details may be obtained from:
Ken Hill Models, Janet Hill Ventures Ltd, Woodfidley Cottage, Brockenhurst, Hants.
Morgan Model Company, Mill Lane, Bulkeley, Malpas, Cheshire.

under these circumstances, and Derek remains annoyed because they aggravated the overall position of deliveries. He is still cagey about revealing the true extent of the waiting list because of this. He remembers the dark days of the mid-sixties when over forty cars stood in dispatch and nobody wanted them, not even on a sale-or-return basis; 'There were cars side-by-side down each edge and double parked down the middle and you couldn't move in there; so nobody need come to me and say "You've had it good all these years," because I know differently; it wasn't always like it is today.' Of such experience is caution born. Some of these cars, like the four-seater coupés, hung around for years, but eventually the tide turned, and the factory, along with dealers, began to sell them off.

For similar reasons, Charles is reluctant to speculate too much about future developments. Obviously he does not mind other people doing so, but points out that whenever customers get wind of a new development, Derek Day has a really bad time of it because many of those in the immediate pipeline want to go for the forthcoming model or modification. Charles is incredulous that companies like Ford can announce a new model so far ahead and still expect to sell the obsolete cars during the lead-in time for the new one. Curiously enough, Derek's experience is to the contrary, in that Morgan customers like the tried and tested, and will plump for a car at the end of a run rather than hold on until a new engine such as the Zeta or 3.9 V8 became available. When the CVH engine was offered with fuel injection and a catalyst, there were still some thirty of the old engines left over; Derek had no problem placing every one of them, and could have

done with more. It was a similar story when the M16 engine was superseded by the T16.

So far the recession in Britain has not bitten too deep at Morgan. But things have changed for the moment. When Derek Day and his agents write to the next twelve customers advising them they can build their cars, they are lucky to get six positive replies. Sometimes there is a 100 per cent positive response, but they may get no replies at all. It averages out at twenty per cent, but there is no pattern. This again makes the waiting list ambiguous: will they or won't they take up their order? Actual cancellations are few, but a number of people have asked for their orders to be deferred until their personal circumstances improve. People's lives can alter radically in six years; they move on, marry, divorce, buy a house, need a family car, and Derek is very much aware of that. Like the car itself, every customer is treated on an individual basis. So there is no complacency at Morgan, despite the six-year waiting list. Peter Morgan would still feel comfortable if the waiting list fell to 18 months, 'Although,' he said, 'if it fell to six months then I would be concerned.' Always be sure demand exceeds supply, HFS advised him.

Peter Morgan is convinced his cars deserve to remain in production, and that some of his father's ideas are still brilliant; he sees Morgan as a specialized marque, not large but strong. He illustrates this by telling me about a Swiss doctor who is now on his fifth Morgan, having ordered his first at the Motor Show in 1962. He keeps his car for about five years and then has another one, selling his old one in Switzerland. At that rate the doctor must be ordering his next car when he takes delivery of the new one!

15 Competition

There is no such thing as the perfect Morgan. They improve with age and evolution, as more data is put back into the mix. This has always been the case, from the first time HFS went trialling with a three-wheeler. Morgans have always been raced; they can be competitive 'straight out of the box', and from the first Le Mans outing in 1938, and the Le Mans and TT Replicas which ensued, the factory has cultivated a competition heritage. The Chris Lawrence-tuned cars of the late 1950s and early 1960s could provide a chapter in Morgan's history on their own, running in long distance sports car races like the Nurburgring 1,000km, Tourist Trophy, Guards Trophy and the GT races which often provided the curtain-raisers to the European Grands Prix. The works-backed Plus 4s of Lawrence and Shepherd-Barron would be up against the likes of Porsche Carrera Abarths in the 1,300cc to 2,500cc class, against smaller-capacity Elites and Giulietta SVZs, with Aston Martin Zagatos and Ferrari 250 GTOs out in front. The Morgan was frequently a class winner in these relatively prestigious events; these were the days when Grand Prix drivers were delighted to race anything. Lawrence teamed up with John Sprinzel in 1964 and went on to build three special Morgan-based SLRs which resembled an Elan crossed with a Marcos. These proved to be astonishingly fast, and Lawrence's marque lap record at the defunct Goodwood circuit still stands. However, an accident in 1966 ended the project, and racing Morgans rather ran out of steam with the passing of the Plus 4's TR4 engine.

Peter Morgan at the wheel of a 4–4 Series 1 at Goodwood in 1948; cycle wing mudguards were used for competition, and fitted after the war when steel was scarce.

Early Competition Successes

Trialling was the sort of competition a driver could pitch his own car into without incurring great expense or risking much damage. It was also a very sociable affair, and Morgans excelled at it. HFS entered his very first 4–4 in the Exeter Trial of 1936 and took the Premier Award, and there was a similar success for a 4–4 in the Edinburgh event that year. In 1938, HFS and Peter Morgan both won Triple Gold Medal awards for completing the Exeter, Land's End and Edinburgh trials without penalty. Morgans continued to do well in trials well into the 1960s.

Before the Second World War, Morgans did well in events such as the RAC Rally, with three consecutive class wins by Works Manager George Goodall from 1937, and his son John winning the 1939 Scottish Rally outright. The emphasis on rallying during the 1950s and early 1960s was to pit the driver's skills against sprints, hill-climbs and driving tests, exercising the navigator's map-reading abilities on road sections. Morgans were ideally suited to these conditions, but with the advent of special stages where ground clearance was vital, Morgan involvement faded.

With the resurgence of classic rallying in the late 1980s, we have seen a growing number of Morgans to the fore once again with people like the Bournes, Barry Taylor and Jim Deacon flying the flag. Back in 1951 when protagonists such as Ian Appleyard in his Jaguar XK120 provided the opposition, Peter Morgan very nearly won the International RAC Rally outright. Morgans took the team prize as consolation, repeating the achievement the following year with Peter Morgan, Jim Goodall, and Dr W. D. Steel driving Vanguard-engined Plus 4s. A lone privateer, Jimmy Ray, won the London Rally in 1952 and 1953; Doc Spare was third in the RAC Rally of 1956 with Pauline Mayman (later a BMC works driver) also showing well in EPM 324. Brian Harper won the 1959 London in his red Plus 4, followed by victory on the Welsh Rally in 1960.

In circuit racing, the 4–4 achieved its first success in 1937 in the hands of Robert Campbell, who won the Ulster Trophy race. The 4–4's reputation was sealed when Prudence Fawcett's works-supported 1,098cc Climax-engined 4–4 finished a fine thirteenth, out of forty-two starters in the 1938 Le Mans 24-hour race. The same car was driven to fifteenth place the following year by Dick Anthony, after he was obliged to run back to the pits for a can of fuel. The next successful attempt at Le Mans was the well-documented Lawrence/Shepherd-Barron GT and 2-litre class win in 1962 with TOC 258. Like Miss Fawcett, they too finished thirteenth overall. There were class wins at Spa and Nurburgring the same year, with the cars of Lawrence, Bill Blydenstein and Pip Arnold finishing first, second and third in the 2.0–2.6-litre class. Possibly the most obscure success was victory in the Panama Grand Prix, a 100-mile event held on an airfield circuit near Panama City. The local agent Pat Kennett dodged a constant hail of gravel thrown up by the E-type/Healey/TR4 opposition and nursed his ailing rear wheel bearings to the finish.

The 1962 Le Mans class-winning Plus 4 Super Sports of Lawrence and Shepherd-Barron, registration TOC 258, is probably the most famous Morgan of all. Raced by Robin Gray in the Charles Spreckley Thoroughbred Championship in 1973 and 1974, it was frequently a winner. In those days I was hardly ever away from race circuits, working weekends in the Brands Hatch Press Office and later doing PR for John Player Team Lotus, as it was known then; I usually managed to watch a lot of races, and could not help but admire this piece of history doing so well against XKs, ACs, 356 Porsches, TRs and the like. TOC 258 certainly made an impression on me.

Robin Gray also ran a modified Lawrence-tuned Plus 8 in ModSports events, and was

BARC Champion in 1974 and class winner in the main series in 1975. From 1980, the owner of TOC 258 was Patrick Keen, who bought the car from Gerry Marshall, and was outright winner of the British Thoroughbred Sports Car Championship in 1981. This category was the successor to 'Marque' racing and a forerunner of classic sports car racing, open to sports cars built before 1960. Opposition came in the form of Jaguar XKs, TRs, Healeys and Aston Martins, and running against modified cars as well in 1982, TOC 258 won its class. In 1984 Keen was second overall in the championship and class winner again.

RUNNERS AND RIDERS

A few years earlier, a Plus 8 was campaigned by Arkley agent John Britten, who managed many class wins in 1975, and Chris Alford, then working at Britten's, easily won the ProdSports championship in a 4/4 with Formula Ford-spec engine the same year. His tally was an impressive class win from each of seventeen starts. In the USA, the 4/4 of Toly Aruntunoff was national production class champion the same year.

Bill Wykeham worked at Morris Stapleton's London agency from 1970, and his racing took off in 1975. By 1978, he was thoroughly competitive, and took a class win in the BRSCC-Aleybars ProdSports series. Bill took Morgans back into the international arena for the first time since 1968 with a special wide-winged Plus 8, built to Group 4 spec by the factory and finished by Bruce Stapleton, and the car was eighteenth in the Brands Hatch Six Hours in 1979. It finished the same event the following year and took part in the Silverstone 1,000km in 1981.

Chris Alford going hard out of the Mallory Park hairpin, keeping ahead of a TR6 during his assault on the 1975 ProdSports championship; he won his class in all seventeen races entered.

Team Normog pose with their cars at Croft in 1974; left to right, *Dick Smith, Plus 4; Sir Aubrey Brocklebank, Plus 4 Super Sports; Andy Garlick, Plus 4; and John Macdonald, Plus 8.*

Bill Wykeham and Ludovic Lindsay take their Super Sports-bodied 1956 Plus 4 through rugged scenery on the Carrera Panamericana; the event lasts eight days and covers 2,000 miles (3,200km).

MMC 11 was the first production Plus 8, starting life in 1968, since when it has had five new chassis and won numerous races and several championships. It is driven by Charles Morgan and Rob Wells, with the latter seen here at Pembrey in July 1992.

The Carrera Panamericana is one of the most exotic long-distance road races in the world. First run in 1950 when the majority of entrants drove large American sedans, the event starts off at Mexico's southern border with Guatemala and runs through vast deserts and scrubland to finish at the Texan border. During the Carrera's eight days and 2,000-mile (3,200km) duration it passes mountains, massive cacti and Aztec ruins. The main consideration is that all the 115 or so starters' cars have to resemble models in existence before 1955. In the mid-fifties, the big European teams including Mercedes Benz, Lancia and Ferrari sent cars for the stars of the time like Ascari and Fangio. A works-supported Scuderia del Portello Alfa Romeo 1900TI saloon won in 1990, and in 1991, Alain de Cadenet's C-type Jaguar replica was the winner. One authentic runner from the event's early days was Bill Wykeham's 1956 Plus 4, with which he finished first in class and fifth overall in 1990, and second in class and fourth overall in 1991. His co-driver was ERA racer Ludovic Lindsay. Amazing results indeed, considering that many of the 'Yank Tanks' had space-frame chassis and modern running gear beneath their period bodies. Bill's car had been rebodied as an aluminium Super Sports by the factory in 1990, its TR3A engine rebuilt by Rick Bourne of Brands Hatch Morgans. I saw a riveting tussle between Bill and Charles Morgan at the 1992 Christies' Meeting at Silverstone, which ended in the latter's favour.

Possibly the most radical racing Plus 8 yet, Rob Wells' winged MMC 3 passing the pits at Silverstone; its wishbone suspension supports a space-frame chassis and one-piece lift-off body.

Charles Morgan's own career in racing took off during the late seventies, with MMC 11 running in production sports car races with an engine blueprinted by Rob Wells of Libra Motive. In 1978 he was outright winner of the DB Motors-sponsored ProdSports series, a separate championship from the one in which Bill Wykeham was

class winner. Charles followed it up as winner of ProdSports Class A in 1979. Rob Wells had previously raced a flat-rad Plus 4 and a fibreglass bodied 4/4 in clubbies, and part of his arrangement with Charles was that he should race MMC 11 when Charles was away wielding his ITN camera. Rob won his class in the DB Motors/Triple C ProdSports

Spectators give Charles and Jane Morgan an enthusiastic reception on the Col de Braus, a Monte Carlo rally stage near Nice, during the 1992 Tour de France; the route also encompassed most of France's major race circuits.

series in 1979, so the car was twice a class winner that year.

With the major components supplied by the factory, Rob Wells built a Plus 8 for the highly modified ModSports championship in 1980. The engine was a special dry-sump V8 from British Leyland Special Tuning, with Weslake heads, and developing some 300bhp. Using a wishbone front suspension set-up, the ensemble was fitted in a special tubular space-frame chassis, and clad in a one-piece lift-off fibreglass body. This was probably the most radical racing Plus 8 ever built, and was the only Morgan ever to have lapped the Silverstone Club circuit in under one minute. Bearing the number plate MMC 3, this car beat all-comers including 911s, Marcos, and hot Elans to win the BRSCC ModSports championship in 1982. Taking ProdSports honours by a whisker in 1982 was Steve Cole in a factory 'assisted' Plus 8, having won twelve out of fifteen races in the Lucas/CAV championship.

Another stalwart of the Morgan racing scene is John Macdonald, joint proprietor of the County Durham agency and race preparation firm, who got his first 4/4 in 1963. This was fitted with a Lea Francis twin-cam engine with an ostentatious chrome-plated side exhaust. He began autotests and sprints with a Plus 4, before succumbing to the lure of 701 HOB, a lightweight Super Sports. With this he could match Cobras and Healeys at his local Croft circuit. In 1973 Macdonalds began their next project, which was a lightweight Plus 8, registration RUP 10M, fitted with one of Allard's development superchargers. Sitting behind 550bhp, John won everything in sight, and resolved to enter two similarly supercharged cars for Le Mans, since the rules for 1974 apparently included a Grand Touring Production class. The race organizers changed their minds, so this very promising project was shelved. Not to be thwarted, John Macdonald set about building one of these cars anyway, and with Development Engineer Maurice Owen's connivance, bought an unused Traco-Oldsmobile V8 from Rover; British Leyland's Competition Department had been racing a Rover P6 3500 using one of these highly tuned engines. The Plus 8

John Macdonald in the fearsome RUP 10M Plus 8 at Croft chicane in 1975. The wings are the widest ever and the air scoop on the bonnet is to accommodate the supercharger.

chassis was clad in an aluminium body with extra-wide wings to accommodate the 8in wide wire wheels, and there were louvres in the inner wings and a large scoop on the bonnet to assist cooling. The resulting machine, OTN 4, was very successful, but John sold it in preference to the feel of the Plus 4, and since 1977 he has developed 550 DXN into a regular class winner.

The Morgan team had often been to the fore in the 750 Motor Club's annual Six-Hour Relay at Silverstone, and there was a renaissance of sorts at Snetterton almost two decades later. From 1980 to 1982, the Morgan Plus 8s covered the greatest distance of any single-car entry in the Willhire 24-Hour race to win the Commander's Cup. This extraordinary event brought together such luminaries of the Morgan world as Mike Duncan, Patrick Keen and Mary Lindsay to form a Morgan Sports Car Club team, while independent entries were the factory's MMC 11 and Morris Stapleton Motors. A similar combination of club team, involving different personnel, and singleton entries turned out for the next two years, with serious crashes for two of the club team cars in 1981. MMC 11 driven by Rob Wells, Chris Alford and Malcolm Paul was outright winner of the event in 1982. The Bulldog Morgan club team using Jim Deacon's car finished fifth in 1983, and in 1984 Mary Lindsay's rebuilt car was placed twelfth. After that, the rules were changed to accommodate saloon cars only.

With a new, purpose-built office and showroom right by the paddock entrance at Brands Hatch, Rick and Jane Bourne have a unique site for their Morgan agency. The couple started rallying XOV 555 in 1990, mainly in national and international events. Most notable was their sixth overall and first in class in that year's Pirelli Classic Marathon, when they were top novices, followed by fifteenth place in 1991. Another car prepared by Brands Hatch Morgans is the Plus 4 four-seater of Barry Taylor, which he shared with Zoë Heritage to take eleventh place on the 1990 Pirelli Classic Marathon. The Bournes were fifth overall and second in class in the RAC International Historic Rally of Great Britain, also in 1991. The next year they managed tenth overall and first in class on this event, and second overall and class winners of the Mitsubishi Classic Marathon. Their car, XOV 555, started life as a 1959 Plus 4, campaigned by Ray Meredith and raced against the likes of Chris Lawrence. Throughout the 1960s, it was developed into one of the fastest Morgans around. There was a period of dereliction after Meredith sold it, until Rick Bourne took it on. Following an accident at Silverstone in 1984, it was fully restored at his old Catford garage to the specification raced by Ray Meredith, and Rick continued to race it enthusiastically in the Morgan challenge series. By 1990, the Bournes had become converted to classic rallying, and XOV 555 was put to different use. Its interior became filled with the all paraphernalia of Jane's navigation equipment.

NATIONAL CHAMPIONSHIP

The national championship for Morgans was originally sponsored by John Millbank's truckhire firm, and the series was won in 1989 and 1990 by Rob Wells in ROB 8R, a road-going Plus 8 built jointly on a smaller 4/4 chassis and frame by the factory and his Libra Motive agency in 1987. In 1991 and 1992 it was running in the hands of Malcolm Paul, who won his class in the 750 Motor Club's RoadSports series. The scheme for 1993 is to fit it with a 360bhp 4.2-litre engine.

For the last three years the series has been sponsored by the factory, administered from 1993 by Assistant Managing Director

Rick and Jane Bourne take a hairpin in their Plus 4 en route to second overall and first in class on the 1992 Mitsubishi Classic Marathon.

Rick and Jane Bourne in 1959 Plus 4 XOV 555 on their mud-spattered way to sixth overall and second in class in the 1992 Rally Britannia.

This Plus 8 was built jointly by Libra Motive and the factory in 1987, using the smaller Plus 4 chassis for better 'chuckability', demonstrated here by Rob Wells at Snetterton's revised Russell corner.

Mark Aston and his wife Serena. There is close contact with all competitors, and cars are prepared by the factory, Morgan agents or specialists. Run over ten rounds at almost all the country's race circuits, there are five classes, each attracting grids of about twenty cars. Class A is for fully-modified Plus 8s, with T16 turbos entering the fray in 1993. Class B is for modified 3.5-litre Plus 8s, Class C for fully modified four-cylinder cars, and Classes D and E for production Plus 8s and four-cylinder cars respectively. Champion in 1991 and 1992 was Chas Windridge, a vet, whose Fiat twin-cam engined Plus 4 ran in Class C. The best attended meeting is the Bentley Drivers' Club Meeting at Silverstone at the end of August, where in 1992 some fifty Morgans were entered for the Tony Morgan-Tipp Memorial race.

Matthew Wurr's car is the fastest Morgan racing, yet ironically it is the least modified in the series. With a standard-chassis car, driven on the road, he was a mere 1.5 seconds off the full-race TVR Tuscans' pace in an inter-marque race at Donington in 1992, and far quicker than sundry 911s and Ferraris. The Morgan has always been a successful racing car because it tends to bend itself to the road surface, enabling suspension geometry to be always pretty much correct, and hence corner fast and predictably. On a bumpy road or rally however, the Morgan is decidedly less at home. But at Donington, Morgans won on handicap. Matthew's car has a Panhard rod and different axle mounting points to negate axle tramp; it is lowered with uprated brakes, springs and dampers, lightened as much as possible, and the engine is highly tuned. The Colin Musgrove and Rob Wells cars are more modified in the suspension department, the latter's having coil springs at the rear instead of leaf springs.

The earth is about to shake as a full grid prepares to depart for a round of the Morgan Challenge held at Silverstone's Bentley Drivers' Club meeting in 1992. Front row comprises Matthew Wurr, Tony Dron, Klaus Nesbach.

Matthew Wurr's 360bhp Class A Plus 8 won the Morris Stapleton trophy for the fastest Morgan of the day at the Bentley Drivers' Club meeting in August 1992.

Competition Models

Customers have always been well catered for with competition versions of 4/4 models; from 1957, output of the Series II competition model's side-valve 100E engine was raised to 40bhp by means of an aluminium inlet manifold, four-branch exhaust and twin SUs. Seven of the thirty-seven cars built to this specification were fitted with aluminium Aquaplane heads. Only three years encompassed the Series III and IV 4/4s, with no competition option, but from 1963 the Series V competition model used the 83.5 bhp Cortina GT engine and twin-choke Weber, high-compression head with high-lift cam, and four-branch exhaust system. It could do 93mph (149km/h) and hit 60mph (96km/h) in 11.9 seconds. The 4/4 1600 competition model of 1969 with its Cortina GT version of the Ford Kent crossflow engine was an improvement. Again, modifications centred on the twin-choke Weber carb and four-branch manifold, raising output to 95.5bhp. Such was the demand for this model that by 1971, all 4/4s were built to the competition specification.

The aluminium-bodied Plus 4 Super Sports came out in 1962 with the regular high-line Plus 4 bonnet, transferring the following autumn to the low-line 4/4 style used and popularized by Chris Lawrence's Le Mans class-winning TOC 258. The chief external difference between Super Sports models and regular Plus 4s was the prominent air scoop with forward facing louvres on the right-hand side of the bonnet, simply riveted onto high-line cars, but properly faired-in subsequently. Although there was a bumper with overriders at the front, there were merely overriders at the rear. Super Sports ran on wide-rim 72-spoke wire wheels, shod with Dunlop RS5 or Duraband competition tyres. Either TR3 or TR4 engines could be specified, depending on whether the intention was to compete in under or over 2.0-litre categories.

Engines were sent away to Lawrencetune in West London for a thorough going over; heads were polished and gas-flowed, high-lift cams complemented the higher 9:1 compression ratio, joined by balanced flywheel, con-rods, crank and clutch, courtesy of Jack Brabham Motors. This heady ensemble was fed by the always visually impressive twin side-draught 42 or 45 DCOE Webers, complete with trumpets, exiting through a four-branch exhaust. Super Sport performance in TR3 guise provided a top speed of 122mph (195km/h) from 115bhp at 5,500rpm, rising to 128mph (205km/h) with the TR4 engine which gave 125bhp at 5,500rpm. Suspension was unchanged from the normal Plus 4, apart from a few which were fitted with telescopic dampers at the rear. A radiator header tank was necessary now because of the low-line bonnet, and an oil cooler was fitted ahead of the radiator. Although by 1968, just 101 Super Sports had been produced, a number of Plus 4 owners subsequently took their cars to Lawrencetune to receive the Super Sports treatment, and the total includes a handful of cars which were exported to the United States with steel bodies and unmodified engines.

Between 1965 and 1967 the factory made forty-two cars known as the Plus 4 Competition. They were based on the Super Sports' low-line body, but lacked the distinctive air intake on the side of the bonnet. These cars were clad in steel instead of aluminium panels, fitted with adjustable Armstrong Selectaride rear dampers, and the only modification to the TR4 engines consisted of a VW Derrington four-branch exhaust system.

WIDER AMBITIONS

Charles Morgan still harbours dreams of another Morgan success at Le Mans, and with the regulations for 1994 allowing production-based sports cars once again, he feels now is the time to give it a go. Whilst it would not be possible to go as fast as a modern Group C sports racer, it may well be feasible to obtain 400bhp; ideally they would need closer to 500bhp. As it is, the car Charles shared with Tony Dron in 1992 was timed at 155mph (248km/h) on the straight at Silverstone. A wing on the back helps downforce at high speed, and this would undoubtedly be a feature of the design. It would probably be a one-off car like MMC 3, but based on a type-approved and homologated chassis, with perhaps one or two copies sold privately. The engine would obviously need to be a full-race unit, and Charles may look further afield than Morgan's current engines, because a Rover V8 fitted with twin turbos would probably fly

apart. The suspension would have to change, because the sliding pillar layout is not adjustable, and such high performance would require fully adjustable wishbone suspension which could be set up for each circuit. The racing Plus 8 is below the weight limit already so it would need to be ballasted.

The essential thing about Morgans is that they are competitive from the word go. At the other end of the scale, Company Secretary Geoff Margetts maintains a Morgan tradition by going trialling with an old red 4/4, which Bill Beck endowed with a 2-litre Fiat twin-cam some ten years ago to provide it with more torque. The factory quite often fields a team of cars for the MMC trials, the Land's End, Edinburgh and Exeter, with Geoff Margetts, Bill Beck and Maurice Owen usually driving.

In the States, John Sheally has dominated the standard production class with his black-and-gold 4/4 for many years; he has been US National Sprint Champion Class C for the last five years. There are also regular

Charles Morgan leads Bill Wykeham during the pair's entertaining tussle at the Christies' meeting, Silverstone, 1992. Charles, driving Mike Duncan's Plus 4 Super Sports, headed Bill's similar car in one race, whilst the order was reversed in another event.

*Still harbouring
dreams of success at
Le Mans, Charles
may take advantage
of new regulations
permitting
production sports
cars to mount an
attack on the 24-
hour epic. The car
he shared with
journalist Tony
Dron, (left), belongs
to Colin Musgrove,
(centre), who looks
relieved to get it
back in one piece; in
1992 it was timed at
155mph (248km/h)
at Silverstone, and
was the only
Morgan running
with fuel injection
and engine
management
system.*

*Morgans are
competitive from the
word go, and club
members have fun at
all levels of the
sport, like this trial
at Pendock, where
the passenger
applies weight to the
nearside rear to get
more traction.*

one-make races for Morgans in the USA, and a series is starting in 1993 in Germany, organized by the Morgan Sports and Racing Car Club of Germany. There is also a flourishing revival of three-wheeler racing, this time against cars as well as bikes. To the fore are Dave Caroline and Stuart Harper, who compete in VSCC events in two-speed Aero Morgans. Stuart won the Dick Seaman Trophy in 1990, and in Post-Vintage events Bill Tuer heads the 1,100cc class both at the circuit and on the hills in an air-cooled Super Sports. I should not forget to mention hillclimbs, since Morgans have always been successful in this branch of the sport; the object is to drive at outrageous speed up little more than tarmac'd farm tracks at places like Shelsley Walsh, Harewood and Doune without falling off the edge, and Mike Hall and Peter Garland have both won the modified roadgoing sports car class numerous times driving Plus 8s in the British Midland Hillclimb Championship. They must be brave men!

Appendix 1

MORGAN AGENTS WORLDWIDE

UK

London
Wykehams Limited
6 Kendrick Place, Reece Mews,
South Kensington SW7 3HF

F. H. Douglass
1a South Ealing Road, Ealing W5 4QT

Libra Motive Limited
2–10 Carlisle Road, Colindale,
London NW9 0HN

Bedfordshire
Allon White & Son Ltd
The Morgan Garage
High Street, Cranfield, Beds
MK43 0BT

Sussex
Robin Kay & Sons
Marine Road, Eastbourne
BN22 7AU

Essex
Cliffsea Car Sales
Bridge Garage, Ness Road,
Shoeburyness SS3 9PG

Berkshire
Mike Spence
Classic Cars Ltd
Unit 1, Bloomfield Hatch,
Mortimer, Reading RG7 3AD

Station Garage
Station Road, Taplow,
Nr. Maidenhead SL6 0NT

Kent
Brands Hatch Morgans
Brands Hatch Circuit
Fawkham, Kent
DA3 8NG

West Midlands
Mike Duncan
250 Ikon Estate, Droitwich Road
Hartlebury, Worcs DY10 4EU

Wiltshire
Burlen Services
Spitfire House, Castle Road,
Salisbury SP1 3SA

Avon
John Dangerfield Garages Ltd
Staplehill Road, Fishponds,
Bristol BS16 5AD

Devon
Phoenix Motors
The Green, Woodbury,
Exeter EX5 1LT

Lancashire
Lifes Motors Ltd
West Street, Southport
PR8 1QN

Cheshire
Donaldson and Evans
The Wolf Garage
Ashley Road, Hale,
Cheshire WA15 9NQ

Yorkshire
Otley Motors
Cross Green, Otley,
West Yorks LS21 1HE

Co. Durham
I & J Macdonald Ltd
Maiden Law Garage, Lanchester
DH7 0QR

Scotland
Parker of Stepps,
Hayston Garage, 38 Glasgow Road,
Kirkintilloch, Glasgow G66 1BJ

Thomson & Potter Ltd
High Street, Burrelton, Blairgowrie,
Perthshire PH13 9NX

Service Facility
Andreas Adamou, Autorapide, Unit 1,
Whitehouse Farm, Cocklake, Wedmore,
N. Somerset BS28 4HE

Overseas

Australia
Calder Sports Car Distributors
Australia Pty Ltd
Box 140 PO
Gisborne 3437, Victoria

Austria
Max Bulla
Liebenstr 40/6/15
A1120 Wien

Belgium
Garage Albert
Anc Ets Stammet Et Fils
S.P.R.L.
84/86 Rue Osseghemstraat
1080 Brussels

Canada
CMC Enterprises (1990) Inc.
RR3 Bolton
Ontario
L7E 5R9

Cyprus
Reliable Sports Cars Ltd
Grivas Digenis Ave
P.O Box 5428
Nicosia

Denmark
Alan Hall
Mollegardsvej 16
GL Hjortkaer
DK-6818 ARRE

France
Jacques Savoye S.A.
237 Boulevard Pereire
75017 Paris

Germany
Merz & Pabst
Alexanderstrasse 46
7000 Stuttgart 1

K. W. Flaving
4750 Unna
Hochstrasse 4

Holland
B. V. Nimag
Reedijk 9 3274 Ke
Heinenoord

Ireland
Scott Macmillan
Holybrooke Hall
Kilmacanogue
Co. Wicklow

Italy
Ditta
Armando Anselmo
Via Vincenzo Tiberio 64
00191 Roma

Japan
Morgan Auto Takano Ltd
9–25 2 Chome Tsumada-
Minami, Atsugi Shi
Kanagawa Ken 243

Luxembourg
Yesteryear Luxembourg
Import Ltd SA
19 Rue Du Parc
L-8083 Bertrange

Norway
Hallan AS
Malmøgt 7
0566 Oslo 5

Portugal
Manuel F Monteiro & Filho
Representacoes e Comércio LDA
Rua Dos Correeiros 71
1100 Lisboa

South Africa
Angela Heinz (Pty) Ltd
6 The Munro Drive
Houghton 2198
P.O. Box 2687
Johannesburg 2000

Spain
Tayre S.A.
Principe de Vergara 253 28016
Madrid

Sweden
A. B. Wendels Bil & Motor
Box 74 Testvagen 10A
S-23200 Arlov

Switzerland
Garage De L'Autoroute
Signy S/Nyon

Rolf Wehrlin
Haupstrasse 132
Aesch BL

United States of America
Isis Imports Ltd
P.O. Box 2290
U.S. Custom House
San Francisco, California 94126

Cantab Motors Ltd
RR1 Box 537A Round Hill
Virginia 22141

Index